Recreation Program Planning Manual for Older Adults

Recreation Program Planning Manual for Older Adults

by Karen Kindrachuk

Venture Publishing, Inc.
State College, Pennsylvania

Venture Publishing, Inc.
1999 Cato Avenue
State College, PA 16801
Phone (814) 234-4561
Fax (814) 234-1651

Production Manager: Richard Yocum
Manuscript Editing: Valerie Fowler, Michele L. Barbin, Shannon B. Dawson, Richard Yocum
Cover by Echelon Design

Library of Congress Catalogue Card Number 2005938307
ISBN-13: 978-1-892132-60-4
ISBN-10: 1-892132-60-5

Table of Contents

Introduction

This manual of program plans is designed to increase direct patient/client care time by providing a selection of programs with a proven track record. All plans were developed and initially implemented with older adults in a long-term care setting. The content of each plan can be applied to any age group.

These plans are designed so that recreation facilitators can implement the program and meet therapeutic needs safely. Each plan has easy-to-read headings that provide quick reference to the concepts behind the plan, preparation, and implementation, as well as specific adaptations with which I have had personal experience. In the next few pages, some general guidelines for implementation will be presented along with a Tips and Tricks section that shares budgetary and manpower secrets.

Remember, the facilitator can make or break the program—groups feed off the energy you provide and clientele will not only evaluate the contents but also how you present the content. I hope you enjoy running these programs as much as I do!

Activity Preparation

Standard practice should include the following:

- List the program on the monthly calendar.
- Use specialty advertisement posters and decorations if necessary.
- Always double check to make sure you have the supplies you need for the program at least one day before. If you have more than one or two people accessing your supply room, what you *thought* was ready and available may have consequently disappeared!
- If program requires individual materials, take enough for two more people than you expect. See Tips and Tricks for resource acquisition ideas.
- Prepare your work area prior to gathering residents for the program (e.g., enough chairs, space for wheelchairs, furniture rearrangement, table setup).

Activity Implementation

Standard practice should include the following:

- Always ensure that all group members have been introduced.
- Explain the purpose and procedure for the particular activity.
- At the end of the program, thank participants for attending and remind them of upcoming programs.

Modifications and Safety Concerns

Standard concerns to keep in mind include the following:

- Social—Encourage each participant to verbally support other players.

- Emotional health of participants—Keep the atmosphere light and fun, especially when implementing competitive programs. Stay positive and redirect any negative comments toward a positive reflection. If dealing with a difficult participant(s), provide a role within the program for that participant (e.g., scorekeeper, candy distributor). Provide encouragement and/or assistance as required to reduce risk of frustration and failure for the participant.

- Hearing—Seat participants with hearing issues beside you with their best ear toward you or seat them in close proximity and lean toward participants, remembering to speak slowly and clearly.

- Difficulty with writing/reading—Assign a scribe to assist with the writing or reading component. Have the participant share their responses or reflections verbally. If dealing with loss of speech also, use a simple word board or Q&A to confirm responses. It may be as simple as providing the participant with a "yes" or "no" word board option or numbered choices to answer trivia questions.

- Materials risk management—Place hot items out of reach, tape down anything that could cause falls, and use chairs with arms and nonskid feet. Think of it this way—if you were entrusting your parent/grandparent to someone else, what safety measures would you expect or suggest?

- Considerations with food-based activities—Know your diets and allergy alerts. Your programs will be one step closer to perfection if preparation is done by an individual who has FoodSafe training.

Volunteers

Useful roles for volunteers include the following:

- Provide topics and have the volunteers compile trivia and create single answer or multiple choice type questions.

- Provide themes or difficulty levels and have the volunteers create word lists for spelling bees.

- Volunteers can help distribute posters/wish lists to various areas in your community.

- Make friends with your local churches. Resources that have come my way include small and large group musical performances; ladies auxiliary volunteer groups; clergy who run chapel services, serve communion, and do 1:1 visits with parishoners. The music resource is invaluable, especially during the Christmas season. Church members (of any affiliation) are a great source to build up religion-based trivia.

- Volunteers can recruit entertainment/outing opportunities through accessing any service groups to which they may personally belong. One of my staff members had her daughter in ballet, so my building was treated to a full ballerina recital by three to six-year olds. A resident belonged to a gardening club previously—a couple of phone calls later we were off to learn about hydroponic gardening. Find out what your family members, staff, and volunteers are involved in and capitalize on their connections!

Tips and Tricks

- Make a wish list and post copies everywhere!
- Make friends with the principals of local elementary schools. Invite them for recitals, visits, to hold a class in conjunction with your participants, to take your participants "back to school" for an afternoon—the possibilities are endless.
- Scrounging is an art, so get good at it. Start calling florists, the library, grocery stores, craft shops (I've found that independent stores are more receptive to giving donations), home decorating stores (wallpaper sample books are a *huge* score), and the like on a regular basis so they get to know your name (taking donuts is always a good bet!). If you need to make purchases, pick your spots and make sure they know you have been supporting them. Drop them wish lists, invite them by for a tour, let them know what you are doing and why. Describe in detail the benefits to your participants. And always, always remember to send a thank-you card for any donation of goods or time you receive—donors appreciate the effort.
- Save everything—even if you don't have a clue what to do with the stuff. If you ask enough people, someone will have an idea of how to use the materials in a program. I have staff saving bread tags off the bread bags—we use them in our scrapbooking sessions, which just goes to show that recreation leaders can find a use for anything under the sun.
- For special events, check out your local party rental store and rent (or ask them to donate, even at a reduced cost is helpful) a cotton candy machine, corndog machine, or snowcone machine. These items can take your event from "fun" to "wow!"

Now get reading and get active!

Section 1
Brain Juice

Brain juice? What the heck is that? Get ready to "hydrate your brain" with a collection of fun cognitive challenges. The brain needs exercise as much as the rest of the body. The old saying "use it or lose it" rings true—and these programs will help to provide cognitive stimulation for all ranges of cognitive levels.

These programs incorporate mental math, long-term and short-term memory, team building skills, and social inclusion, all in a fun, learning environment. Help to enrich vocabulary with the Old Fashioned Spelling Bee. Practice skills like patience and teamwork in Survival. Learn something new through trivia questions.

So break out those thinking caps, take out your pens and paper, and have some fun!

SURVIVAL

Objective

To increase cognitive stimulation and learning through friendly competition

Targeted Domains and Benefits

Cognitive	problem solving, abstract thinking, memory recall
Social	cooperation, team playing, support for others
Emotional	sense of accomplishment, increased self-esteem

Preparation and Materials

- ballots with animal names (3 of each) for team division exercise (optional)
- a pen or pencil per team
- a copy of each exercise per team
- a roll of tape per team
- newspapers to share

Scoring Procedure

1st team to finish	4 points
2nd team to finish	3 points
3rd team to finish	2 points
4th team to finish	1 point
Speed bonus	1 point

Rules: If a team finishes before time is up, they will receive one bonus point. After time is called, points awarded are decided by the amount of correct answers on each team's exercise sheet. Any team may finish before time is up. If this happens, all areas of the exercise must be filled in. Otherwise, the team must continue with the exercise until time is up. Points for team creation exercise are at the leader's discretion, or as suggested.

Procedure

1. Using the animal ballots, have each individual act out (charades with noises allowed) their particular ballot. Participants must

discover others acting out the same animal. These three participants are then a "survivor" team. Mark which team is gathered first.

2. The first exercise is Brain Boosters. Allow ten minutes for completion. Mark down the order in which teams finish (see scoring scale). Teams are allowed to finish as quickly as possible with no penalty, but if finished early they must have completed the entire exercise (no blanks).

3. The second exercise is Word Scramble. The time allowed is at the leader's discretion, but ten minutes is suggested. Mark down the order in which teams finish (see scoring scale). Teams are allowed to finish as quickly as possible with no penalty, but if finished early they must have completed the entire exercise (no blanks).

4. The third exercise is Newspaper Sculpture. Hand out old newspapers to each team, accompanied by a roll of tape (scotch or masking). Assign each team one of the animals from the word scramble list. Explain to participants that they have ten minutes in which to create their assigned animal using only newspaper, tape, and their team members. Scoring can be determined two ways: a) each team will receive equal points based on participation or b) have a different staff member assist in judging—the alternate staff member can determine which sculpture looks most like the assigned animal, then almost like, and then a completely original animal, with the scoring as before for 1st, 2nd, 3rd and 4th. This round usually provides the most hilarity.

5. Once all the exercises have been completed, tally the scores for the four groups. Have four small prizes, one for each group member. (My suggestion: a fake check, made out in four different amounts). Thank all participants for coming and encourage future attendance.

Modifications

Physical
Parkinson's/MS/Loss of or reduced vision: Ensure that each group has one person who can scribe/read aloud for the team, or assign a volunteer to fill this role.

Cognitive
This program is most appropriate for high-functioning participants. In the event of using this program with midrange cognitive functioning, the facilitator can delete or replace questions to ensure greater group success. The Word Scramble has worked with some midrange functioning participants

but works better when used as a spelling bee type of activity, having participants spell the word versus unscrambling it.

Social/Emotional

For participants exhibiting negative social interactions, run this program with a reduced number of participants, using the first challenge as an independent exercise. Create a two-person team for the second exercise and a three-person team for the third exercise.

Safety Issues

- Make sure that the tape used in the newspaper exercise does not directly adhere to any exposed skin or wound wrappings.

Tips and Tricks

- Load up on candy after Halloween, Easter, and Christmas. The bite-sized bars make a great prize. The chocolate stays fresh for some time if you double bag it and put it in the freezer right away. Ask local retailers to donate a bag or two after the holiday has passed.

Brain Boosters (Nature)

1. What bear weighs up to 1700 pounds?
2. What formation do Canada Geese fly in?
3. What is a female black bear called?
4. What is the largest rodent in North America?
5. Which bear can climb trees?
6. Beaver babies are called what?
7. Cougars attack their prey from which direction?
8. How fast can a black bear run?
9. When camping, how high does food need to be hung in the air to avoid attracting animals?
10. To which area/continent is the cougar (or mountain lion) native?
11. How tall is a giraffe?
12. How many vertebrae does a giraffe have in its neck?
13. What animal is prickly and rolls itself into a ball?
14. Where did black bears originate?
15. What animal has a wide, flat tail used for balance and swimming?
16. What are the common wintering areas of the Canada Goose?
17. Are giraffes herbivores or carnivores?
18. What is the coloring of the Canada Goose?
19. How do beavers waterproof their dams?
20. What bear fishes for salmon?

Answers for Brain Boosters (Nature)

1. Grizzly Bear
2. "V" formation
3. Sow
4. Beaver
5. Black bear
6. Kits
7. Behind
8. 50 km/h
9. 9 feet (3 meters)
10. North America
11. 18 feet
12. 7
13. Hedgehog
14. Asia
15. Beaver
16. Cities, Golf Courses
17. Herbivores
18. White/Black/Tan
19. Mud
20. Grizzly Bear

Word Scramble (Nature)

1. cetaheh
2. rgocua
3. pleenhat
4. nigat nadap
5. ryzizlg ebra
6. akaol reba
7. xynl
8. lapro erab
9. muap
10. nhosroecir
11. giret
12. evlinrewo
13. vwloes
14. firfaeg
15. teiliwath eder
16. esomo
17. pohgre
18. klbac erba
19. gdeohgeh
20. pigaem
21. vebaer
22. naletpoe
23. cnecihk
24. rdaople
25. reosh

Answers for Word Scramble (Nature)

1. Cheetah
2. Cougar
3. Elephant
4. Giant Panda
5. Grizzly Bear
6. Koala Bear
7. Lynx
8. Polar Bear
9. Puma
10. Rhinoceros
11. Tiger
12. Wolverine
13. Wolves
14. Giraffe
15. Whitetail Deer
16. Moose
17. Gopher
18. Black Bear
19. Hedgehog
20. Magpie
21. Beaver
22. Antelope
23. Chicken
24. Leopard
25. Horse

Brain Boosters (Farming)

1. What animal can you see on a farm that looks like a dog, but isn't a wolf?
2. What is used to swath a field?
3. Standing sheaves in a vertical pile is called...?
4. Are horseshoes stapled or nailed onto the hooves of horses?
5. What instrument was used to call the family/workers in for meal times?
6. What club do children on farms usually belong to?
7. What was a house made of earth called?
8. Before indoor plumbing, what was used as a bathroom?
9. What was the name of the large 2-wheeled cart usually pulled by oxen?
10. What hand tool was used to cut grain?
11. What type of plow was used by one man and one ox/horse?
12. What was is called when the local community gathered together to build a barn?
13. What is a famous type of country dancing?
14. This was used this to make butter.
15. What type of soap was traditionally used in washing clothes?
16. What was used to sharpen a razor?
17. How many rooms did the schoolhouse usually contain?
18. What hand tool was used in threshing grain?
19. What was the name given to a car pulled by horses?
20. This is where all the preserves were usually stored.

Answers for Brain Boosters (Farming)

1. Coyote
2. Combine
3. Stooking
4. Nailed
5. Triangle
6. 4-H
7. A sod-house or "soddie"
8. Outhouse
9. Red River Cart
10. Scythe
11. One bottom plow
12. Barn-Raising
13. Square Dancing
14. Butter Churn
15. Lye
16. Razor Strop
17. One
18. Flail
19. Bennett Buggy
20. Root Cellar

Word Scramble (Farming)

1. bmoince
2. ocw
3. setlba
4. ranb
5. ldfei
6. nceef
7. dwbebareri
8. tsaex aget
9. cnehikc cpoo
10. gpnepi
11. ecllayddse
12. dseew
13. rwtheea
14. hlai rmsto
15. mpuerb orcp
16. ylaofht
17. cyoowb
18. arnch
19. lttaec
20. ntaernl
21. utbret lomd
22. gdaern
23. lwel
24. agncnin
25. lops plia

Answers for Word Scramble (Farming)

1. Combine
2. Cow
3. Stable
4. Barn
5. Field
6. Fence
7. Barbed Wire
8. Texas Gate
9. Chicken Coop
10. Pigpen
11. Clydesdale
12. Weeds
13. Weather
14. Hail Storm
15. Bumper Crop
16. Hayloft
17. Cowboy
18. Ranch
19. Cattle
20. Lantern
21. Butter Mold
22. Garden
23. Well
24. Canning
25. Slop Pail

Show Me the Money

Objective

To increase cognitive stimulation and learning through friendly competition

Targeted Domains and Benefits

Cognitive	problem solving, memory recall, active learning
Social	cooperation, team playing, support for others
Emotional	sense of accomplishment, increased self-esteem and self-confidence

Preparation and Materials

- fake money in denominations of $50, $100, $500, $1000, $5000, $10,000, $50,000, $100,000 or blank "checks" to write out to the winners (see samples in Appendix).
- a copy of each game activity sheet
- a pen or pencil and pad of paper for keeping score

Procedure

1. Choose whether the group will participate in teams (recommended if more than eight participants) or as individuals.
2. Read the question, then read aloud all four answers (the answer in bold is the correct answer) and have participants select which answer they think is correct.
3. Once all the exercises have been completed, tally the scores and award prizes (see scoring procedure). Thank all participants for attending and encourage future attendance.

Modifications

Physical

When using this program with the hearing impaired, have a volunteer sit near the participants to repeat question as required, or seat participants in front of the facilitator. Optional format: Provide a written outline of questions and possible answers for participants to read.

Cognitive
This program is most appropriate for high-functioning participants. If using with mid-range cognitive functioning levels, the facilitator can delete or re-place questions to provide for greater group success.

Social/Emotional
For participants exhibiting negative social interactions, run this program with a reduced number of participants. Encourage positive support between all group members. If participants become frustrated or make negative comments to other group members, give gentle prompts as to socially appropriate behaviors. If the behavior continues, have the disruptive participant take a leadership role (e.g., read questions out loud for you, keep score if able).

Safety Issues

Damaging Self-Confidence/Self-Esteem
Ensure that you give participants a chance to answer—or to pass—and record their answers/scores accordingly.

Tips and Tricks

- Do not hesitate to ask seemingly difficult questions—you will be surprised what some people know. Besides, it is an opportunity for participants to learn something new.
- Using the fake money as a "prize" is a great incentive for participation for higher functioning participants. Have participants save their accumulated winnings and then hold a small "auction" with donated prizes/gifts that they can then use their "money" to bid on.

Scoring Procedure

There are two scoring options: individual or group/team. Each strategy is outlined next.

Individual

1. If possible, seat participants in a semi-circle, facing the facilitator.
2. On the paper, make a column for participants with their names at the top. Make a list from 1—10 in each column (if done on the computer; the facilitator then only has to fill in names—a bit of a timesaver!)
3. Ask each question, and give each participant a chance to answer.
4. Keep track of who has the right answer—these participants will receive the full monetary value of the question.

5. Put the question's value amount beside the corresponding number in the column of participants who answered correctly.

6. For participants selecting the incorrect answer, an honorary $50 should be indicated beside the corresponding number in their column.

7. At the end of the questions, total up the winnings for each participant.

8. Prizes can consist of fake checks made out to each participant for their total amount, or hand out fake money in the winning amount.

Group/Team

1. Group each team of participants with a distinct space in between (if possible), or seat them at separate tables.

2. Have the team pick a name. Try to have this team stay together for at least four consecutive programs, then switch participants around (if using a monthly rotation plan).

3. Make a column on the paper for each team and place their name at the top. Make a list from 1–10 in each column (if this is done on the computer, then the facilitator only has to fill in names—a bit of a timesaver!).

4. After asking the question, allow the team to confer before providing a common agreed-upon answer.

5. Keep track of who has the correct answer—these teams will receive the full monetary value of the question.

6. Put the question's value amount beside the corresponding number in the column of participants who answered correctly.

7. For teams selecting the incorrect answer, an honorary $50 should be indicated beside the corresponding number in their column.

8. At the end of the questions, total up the winnings for each team.

9. Prizes can consist of fake checks made out to each participant for their total amount, or hand out fake money in the winning amount.

Game One

Question #1—$100
What bird is believed to have risen from its own ashes?
　　Ostrich
　　Phoenix
　　Raven
　　Sparrow

Question #2—$200
When you are playing the piano, you are tickling the . . .
　　Keys
　　Ivories
　　Tune
　　Funny Bone

Question #3—$300
This famous actress sang "Happy Birthday" to President JFK:
　　Merle Oberon
　　Bette Davis
　　Greta Garbo
　　Marilyn Monroe

Question #4—$500
Which U.S. state borders Canada?
　　Louisiana
　　Kansas
　　Utah
　　North Dakota

Question #5—$1000
What religious group did Brigham Young lead to Utah?
　　Mormons
　　Seventh Day Adventists
　　Catholics
　　Scientologists

Question #6—$2000
What natural hazard is most feared in Switzerland?
　　Flood
　　Earthquake
　　Avalanche
　　Blizzard

Question #7—$4000
How many arms does a Starfish have?
  2
  3
  5
  8

Question #8—$8000
Which country's name means "rich coast"?
  Costa Rica
  El Salvador
  Barbados
  Peru

Question #9—$16,000
The Transylvanian Alps can be found in this country:
  Romania
  Transylvania
  Canada
  France

Question #10—$32,000
What woman in the Bible married Boaz?
  Esther
  Ruth
  Jezebel
  Eve

Question #11—$64,000
Which of these vegetables has poisonous leaves?
  Potato
  Rhubarb
  Radish
  Beets

Question #12—$125,000
What is the oldest sport in North America?
  Hockey
  Golf
  Lacrosse
  Football

Question #13—$250,000
The mandible is found in this part of the body:
> **Head**
> Arms
> Legs
> Torso

Question #14—$500,000
Who wrote the 1812 Overture?
> Beethoven
> **Tchaikovsky**
> Mozart
> Bach

Question #15—$1,000,000
This was one thing Marco Polo *did not* bring back from the East:
> Nutmeg
> Cloves
> Pepper
> **Vanilla**

Game Two

Question #1—$100
How many playing cards are there in a standard deck of cards (not including jokers)?
 50
 52
 54
 48

Question #2—$200
Scottish men wear a skirt called a:
 Tam
 Kilt
 Sporran
 Crinoline

Question #3—$300
This famous 1940s actor starred in "Casablanca":
 Rudolph Valentino
 Humphrey Bogart
 Paul Newman
 Robin Williams

Question #4—$500
Which city is known as "The City of Light?"
 Paris
 Rome
 New York
 Amsterdam

Question #5—$1000
The giant panda inhabits which country?
 England
 China
 Australia
 India

Question #6—$2000
Who is the author of *Treasure Island* and *The Strange Case of Dr. Jekyll and Mr. Hyde*?
>   Alex Haley
>   **Robert Louis Stevenson**
>   Mark Twain
>   Lewis Carroll

Question #7—$4000
What item do Americans throw out in the greatest quantity?
>   Food
>   Tires
>   **Paper**
>   Cloth

Question #8—$8000
How many toe pads does a cat have on each of its back paws?
>   **4**
>   5
>   3
>   6

Question #9—$16,000
What is a dromedary?
>   Mule
>   **Camel**
>   Desert Dog
>   Scorpion

Question #10—$32,000
What is the shortest day in the Northern Hemisphere (also referred to as the Winter Solstice)?
>   December 30
>   **December 21**
>   November 24
>   December 1

Question #11—$64,000
Which planet is so large it could contain all the others?
    Neptune
    Uranus
    Mars
    Jupiter

Question #12—$125,000
What ingredient for pasta dishes did Columbus bring back from his travels to the "New World"?
    Garlic
    Tomatoes
    Mushrooms
    Cheese

Question #13—$250,000
The sari is traditional clothing for women of which country?
    Japan
    Egypt
    India
    Iran

Question #14—$500,000
The gorse shrub has this color of flowers:
    Purple
    White
    Blue
    Yellow

Question #15—$1,000,000
Which is a French word that means "twice cooked"?
    Biscuit
    Blasé
    Flambé
    Sear

Game Three

Question #1—$100
According to the Bible, a whale swallowed this person:
- Isaiah
- **Jonah**
- Lot
- Sarah

Question #2—$200
Who was Sherlock Holmes's faithful sidekick?
- Wadsworth
- Walker
- Houdini
- **Watson**

Question #3—$300
In the movie *The Sound of Music* Maria's occupation before she became governess was:
- Washerwoman
- Shepherdess
- **Nun**
- Musician

Question #4—$500
Which emotion is known as the green-eyed monster?
- Love
- **Jealousy**
- Hate
- Apathy

Question #5—$1000
In which country would you find the Sinai Desert?
- **Egypt**
- Ethiopia
- Saudi Arabia
- Iraq

Question #6—$2000
Which is NOT a gambling game?
    Poker
    Roulette
    Backgammon
    Patience

Question #7—$4000
The drug opium is produced from this flower:
    Daisy
    Hyacinth
    Dandelion
    Poppy

Question #8—$8000
In which country was Chopin born?
    Ukraine
    Poland
    Czech Republic
    Bavaria

Question #9—$16,000
Literary hero The Scarlet Pimpernel aided in the escape of aristocracy from which country?
    Belgium
    Norway
    France
    Germany

Question #10—$32,000
Castles were originally built as:
    Demonstration of family wealth & power
    Tourist attractions
    Defensive forts
    Multiple family dwellings

Question #11—$64,000
Which of these countries does the equator *not* go through?
    Zaire
    Argentina
    Kenya
    Brazil

Question #12—$125,000
Which is *not* a measurement of length:
   Cubic foot
   Mile
   Meter
   Inch

Question #13—$250,000
In which book did Scout go to a school pageant dressed as a ham?
   Adventures of Huckleberry Finn
   Tom Sawyer
   Catcher in the Rye
   To Kill a Mockingbird

Question #14—$500,000
What woman of the Bible was a Jewish commoner, married a king, and saved her people from persecution?
   Ruth
   Esther
   Bathsheba
   Mary

Question #15—$1,000,000
Neptune's trident appears on the flag of which country?
   Greece
   Barbados
   Crete
   Jamaica

Game Four

Question #1—$100
In what year did the Titanic sink?
   1920
   1912
   1915
   1913

Question #2—$200
What year was the attack on Pearl Harbor?
   1940
   1943
   1944
   1941

Question #3—$300
What is it called when you knit one row and purl the next?
   Beginner's stitch
   Stockinette stitch
   Argyle stitch
   Cable stitch

Question #4—$500
Which country is *not* in North America?
   Mexico
   Canada
   Columbia
   United States

Question #5—$1000
Most people in the world are killed by:
   Floods
   Drought
   Earthquakes
   Volcanoes

Question #6—$2000
This plant was the first crop to make money in colonial America:
   Coffee
   Cotton
   Peanuts
   Tobacco

Question #7—$4000
Which is NOT a fossil fuel?
Wood
Coal
Oil
Natural Gas

Question #8—$8000
A thermal spring has water that is:
Hot
Warm
Cool
Cold

Question #9—$16,000
What is the second largest French-speaking city (not in France)?
Amsterdam
Montreal
Antwerp
Cape Town

Question #10—$32,000
Ocean tides are created by:
Poseidon
The Sun
The Moon
Ocean Currents

Question #11—$64,000
Who discovered the antibiotic penicillin?
Louis Pasteur
Marie Curie
Pierre Berton
Sir Alexander Fleming

Question #12—$125,000
Where does mohair yarn come from?
Goats
Mice
Sheep
Horses

Question #13—$250,000
Ukrainian women dancers traditionally wear boots of this color:
    White
    Black
    Red
    Blue

Question #14—$500,000
The first settlers of Australia were:
    French
    Canadian
    American
    British

Question #15—$1,000,000
This man was the Hudson Bay's first inland explorer:
    Henry Kelsey
    Henry Hudson
    Henry Baker
    Henry Cabot

OLD FASHIONED SPELLING BEE

Objective

To increase long-term and short-term memory, sequencing skills, and learning through friendly competition

Targeted Domains and Benefits

Cognitive   problem solving, memory recall, active learning

Social   cooperation, team playing, support for others

Emotional   sense of accomplishment, increased self-esteem and self-confidence

Preparation and Materials

- fake money in denominations of: $50, $100, $500, $1000, $5000, $10,000, $50,000, $100,000 or blank checks to write out to the winners (see samples in Appendix)
- bite-sized chocolate bars
- a pen or pencil per team
- a piece of paper per team
- whiteboard/marker or chalkboard/chalk

Procedure

1. Choose whether the group will participate in teams or as individuals. If playing in individual format, have a group size of six maximum or it becomes an exercise in frustration for team members (and the facilitator!). Have teams sit at separate tables (if possible), or in the same general location (group chairs). Toss a coin to determine which team starts the program (if playing as individuals, choose from the right or the left, as an easy option).

2. The facilitator reads the word aloud—one option is to use the word in a sentence (the "recovery" point is then obsolete—see Tips and Tricks for recovery point option).

3. Each team has 30 seconds to discuss the word and 30 seconds to write or verbally provide the correct spelling. If using the verbal option, the facilitator writes down each letter as the team says it to avoid any protests from the other team. The designated time can

be altered to suit participants' processing/verbalization times and requirements.

4. For each correctly spelled word, the team receives one point. Alternately, in the event of a misspelling the facilitator can allow the other team to "steal" the answer. If the opposing team spells the word correctly, they will receive that point. The team at the end of the spelling list with the most points is the winner.

Modifications

Physical

This option works very well with the visually impaired—as long as they have had some experience with the written word. It also works very well with participants who experience any physical difficulty (e.g., Parkinson's, stroke, MS). If they are unable to write, they can participate verbally within the group and/or as the team answer person, either independently or by reading the answer that the team has written out.

Cognitive

This program is most appropriate for high-functioning participants. If using with mid-range cognitive functioning levels, the facilitator can delete or replace words to provide for greater group success.

Social/Emotional

Encourage positive support among all group members. If participants become frustrated or make negative comments to other group members, give gentle prompts as to socially appropriate behaviors. If the behavior continues, have the disruptive participant take a leadership role (e.g., read questions out loud for you, score keep if able).

Safety Issues

See the "recovery point" option under Tips and Tricks. Allow enough time for each team to feel that they have ample opportunity to come to a group consensus regarding the answer/spelling.

Tips and Tricks

- Do not hesitate to use words that are uncommon—or more than two syllables—you will be surprised what some people know. Besides, it is an opportunity for participants to learn something new.
- If using this program with an Alzheimer's group, use phonics cards (2 sets) and have them pull out the one that matches the one you are holding up or describing.

- To keep the "success for all" concept in place, if a team does not answer correctly, spell the word for them and then give the definition. For a "recovery" point, ask them to use it correctly in a sentence.
- Experience has shown that small snack-type treats (especially chocolate) are a great incentive in this activity!

Spelling List One

1. Brain — You use your *brain* every day.

2. Sleep — Every night you go to *sleep*.

3. Basket — Moses was found floating down the river in a *basket*.

4. Choice — Make your *choice*.

5. Range — Cows live out on the *range*.

6. Forest — You can't see the *forest* for the trees.

7. Ideal — He was an *ideal* husband.

8. Quickly — You must move *quickly*.

9. Passive — He made a *passive* offer of help.

10. Relative — Everyone has a *relative* they'd rather not have.

11. Abscond — The thief intended to *abscond* with the painting.

12. Capable — She was *capable* of getting better marks in school.

13. Paternal — She was my *paternal* aunt.

14. Reluctant — The girl was *reluctant* to accept a date with that fellow.

15. Moniker — Big Betty was the *moniker* given to the girl who was 7 feet tall.

16. Diligently — The scientist applied himself *diligently* to his work.

17. Radiator — My car's *radiator* started leaking.

18. Multiple — The test was a *multiple* choice test.

19. Fluctuate — The temperature will *fluctuate* over the next week.

20. Ancient — Egyptian mummies are *ancient*.

21. Progressive — I attended the *progressive* supper last evening.

22. Balustrade — I could see the entire ballroom from behind the *balustrade*.

23. Temporary — It's only a *temporary* set-back.

24. Exquisite — The diamond necklace was *exquisite*.

25. Alias — The spy used an *alias* while on a mission.

26. Commitment — Marriage requires a *commitment*.

27. Emissary — The pope sent an *emissary* to the Arctic.

28. Congruent — Two triangles are *congruent* to each other.

29. Synchronized — The racers *synchronized* their watches before the race started.

30. Illuminate — You turn on a light to *illuminate* a room.

Spelling List Two

1. Relate — Who can *relate* to my story?
2. Inform — The doctor will *inform* you of your problem.
3. Rash — He made a *rash* decision.
4. Immediate — I need an *immediate* reply.
5. Reflection — I saw my *reflection* in the pool.
6. Gesture — That driver made a rude *gesture* in my direction.
7. Lease — I had to sign a *lease* on my apartment.
8. Mammal — A cow is a *mammal*.
9. Nostril — A nose has a *nostril* on each side.
10. Predator — A wolf is *predator* of the wild.
11. Occupation — A student must think about an *occupation*.
12. Sedate — They had to *sedate* the patient in the hospital.
13. Triplicate — Each form needs to be filled out in *triplicate*.
14. Uneven — Since last winter, the sidewalk has been *uneven*.
15. Venom — A snake's *venom* is dangerous.
16. Fusion — The blending or melting of two things is *fusion*.
17. Delegate — I will *delegate* some of my duties.
18. Jacket — I need my *jacket* to stay warm.
19. Prevalent — Traveling is quite *prevalent* in Europe.
20. Knickers — Golfers wear *knickers* as part of their outfit.
21. Hibernate — Bears *hibernate* every winter.
22. Giraffe — A *giraffe* only has seven vertebrae in its neck.
23. Dowager — The *dowager* lived in the mansion on the hill.
24. Coerce — I'll try to *coerce* that person to buy insurance.
25. Limousine — The wedding party rode in a *limousine*.
26. Penance — The priest assigned a Hail Mary as *penance*.
27. Lucrative — It was a *lucrative* business deal.
28. Virulent — This illness is particularly *virulent*.
29. Cartouche — The Egyptian king's *cartouche* contained his name in hieroglyphics.
30. Assimilate — When we eat vegetables, we *assimilate* the vitamins into our body.

BIBLE TRIVIA

Objective

To increase long-term and short-term memory and provide religious comfort through remembering Bible stories related to trivia answers

Targeted Domains and Benefits

Cognitive	problem solving, memory recall, active learning
Social	cooperation, team playing, support for others
Emotional	sense of accomplishment, increased self-esteem and self-confidence
Spiritual	facilitating spiritual comfort by recall of Bible stories related to trivia answers

Preparation and Materials

- jellybeans
- small bowls for jellybeans
- a pen or pencil and pad of paper for keeping score
- copy of trivia questions

Procedure

1. Choose whether the group will participate in teams or as individuals. If choosing the individual format, have a group size of six maximum or it becomes an exercise in frustration for team members (and for the facilitator!). Have teams sit at separate tables (if possible), or in the same general location (group the chairs). Toss a coin to determine which team starts the program (if playing as individuals, choose from the right or the left, as an easy option).

2. Provide each participant or group with a pen and paper. Write team names on the top of each paper.

3. The facilitator reads the trivia question aloud. Each team has 30 seconds to discuss the question and 30 seconds to write down their answer. At the one-minute mark, each team must hand in their answer sheet to the facilitator who will then read each team's answer aloud. The designated time can be altered to suit participants' processing, verbalization, or writing time and requirements.

4. For each correct answer, place two jellybeans in that team's bowl—one jellybean in the bowl in the event of an incorrect answer. In theory, each team could "win" two jellybeans per answer, but at the least each team will have some candy accumulated by game's end!

Modifications

Physical

This activity works very well with the physically impaired, as all they need is the ability to verbalize their responses to team members. Have those with speaking difficulties scribe the answers for their team, if they are able to write. In the event of using a communication board, prepare a specific board (computerized or hand-drawn) with the answers, plus a few wrong answers, and then present the temporary communication board to the participant. MRSA participants will need to have their jellybeans put into a separate dish to allow for proper infection control procedures.

Cognitive

This program is most appropriate for high-functioning participants. If using with mid-range cognitive functioning levels, the facilitator can focus the program to be more learning-based than recall-based. Ask if they can tell the story pertaining to the questions and answers versus just providing an answer to the question. Remember the cohort—many of this generation grew up attending church and will probably know much more than you expect!

Social/Emotional

Encourage positive support between all group members. If participants become frustrated or make negative comments to other group members regarding religious beliefs, use the behavior as an opportunity to discuss tolerance and acceptance of others. It can be an eye-opening experience to jump from trivia to life-skills coaching!

Safety Issues

Group Conflict

Participants may have a variety of religious backgrounds. If conflict arises (negative connotations toward other members, or the provided question) take a breather for a tolerance and sensitivity in-service. Offer the aggressor an opportunity at the end of the program to provide "bonus" questions, based on their religious beliefs, to the rest of the group.

Tips and Tricks

- Check with local churches—they may have already prepared this type of material to use with their own groups (especially the children's groups). They may be willing to share and perhaps even have a book they're willing to lend out on a regular basis from the church library. You could possibly recruit a church member to compile the information for you and in the process recruit a regular volunteer for your facility.

- The team format works very well for this particular program—and the collective jellybeans are a great hit after the program. If you finish early, the participants can enjoy their snack and the facilitator can use that time to further reminisce about past church experiences. Note: in the event of diabetic issues, it's always best to try to get sugar-free treats.

- To make things interesting (and if your policies and procedures say nothing about "gambling"), you can allow teams to "double or nothing" prior to a question. If they choose this option, and answer correctly, they receive four jellybeans. If the answer is incorrect, they receive no jellybeans.

Bible Trivia

1. What child was put in a basket to float down the Nile?
   Moses

2. What was the name of Moses' sister?
   Miriam

3. Who built the ark?
   Noah

4. What bird showed Noah the floodwaters had receded?
   Dove

5. Who had the coat of many colors?
   Joseph

6. How many tribes of Israel were there?
   12

7. Who was swallowed by a whale?
   Jonah

8. What evil Queen was thrown over the wall and eaten by dogs as punishment?
   Jezebel

9. How many of each animal did Noah take into the ark?
   2

10. Joshua's army marched around the walls of Jericho for how long before the walls collapsed?
    7 days

11. What woman ended up marrying Boaz, a rich local farmer?
    Ruth

12. Who had long hair and immeasurable strength?
    Samson

13. Who was the wisest king and built a great and beautiful temple?
    Solomon

14. What book in the Bible contains a collection of wise sayings?
    Proverbs

15. What verse (book, chapter, verse) starts with "For God so loved the world..."?
    John 3:16

16. The book of Isaiah is found in which part of the Bible?
    Old Testament

17. Whose wife was turned into a pillar of salt?
    Lot's

18. Who saw the burning bush in the wilderness?
Moses

19. Who was thrown into the lion's den?
Daniel

20. Who was the oldest man in the Bible?
Methuselah

21. How many books are in the New Testament?
27

22. What are the first four books of the New Testament?
Matthew, Mark, Luke, John

23. What are the two books in the Bible named after women?
Ruth, Esther

24. What was Babylon famous for?
The Hanging Gardens

25. Who were the three men thrown into the fiery furnace?
Shadrach, Meshach, and Abednego

26. How many times did Peter deny Jesus?
3

27. How many pieces of silver did Judas receive for betraying Jesus?
30

28. Who took over as leader of Israel after Moses died?
Joshua

29. What was the name of the bread the Israelites ate in the desert while leaving Egypt?
Manna

30. Who was the first man to die in the Bible?
Abel

31. How long did Jacob have to work to make Rachel his wife?
14 years

32. Who was the king when Jesus was born?
Herod

33. What woman hid the two spies sent by Joshua to view the land?
Rahab

CONCENTRATION

Objective

To increase long-term and short-term memory and to demonstrate short-term recall

Targeted Domains and Benefits

Cognitive	problem solving, memory recall, active learning
Social	cooperation, team playing, support for others
Emotional	sense of accomplishment, increased self-esteem and self-confidence

Preparation and Materials

- variety of objects in a container to take with you
- 2 trophies/medals
- tent cards with numbers corresponding to the objects used
- a pen or pencil per team
- a piece of paper per team
- selection of objects to use during the game
- dish towels, hand towels, or boxes to cover the objects

Procedure

1. Choose whether the group will participate in teams or as individuals. If choosing the individual format, have a group size of five maximum to maintain a medium challenge-level.
2. Have all participants sit around the table, providing an unobstructed view of the objects. If playing in team format, ensure that team members are sitting beside each other.
3. Each participant or group is provided with a pen and paper to write their team answers. Make sure team/individual names are on the paper.
4. Have participants close their eyes while you place the objects on the table—make sure to number the objects so there is no confusion!
5. On your count, have participants open their eyes and begin a timed viewing (e.g., 60 seconds) of the objects. When time is up, have them close their eyes and cover the objects.

6. When the objects are covered again, each participant opens their eyes and writes down each object they remember, according to the number beside each object (e.g., #1 is a clock, #2 is hand cream). Provide each team with a time frame in which to write down their answers to each number.

7. After time is called, uncover the objects and compare each team/ individual answer. Tally team/individual points on your own scorecard—award one point for every correct answer. At the end of your round(s), tally the points and award a 1st and 2nd place trophy or ribbon to the team/individual.

8. Recycle the trophies month to month (use accumulated monthly points and hand out the trophy at the end of each month), or award ribbons/medals at the end of each program.

Modifications

Physical

This program works very well for anyone with a physical impairment, as all they need is the ability to verbalize their response to team members. Have those with speaking difficulty scribe the answer for their team, if they are able to write. In the event of using a communication board, prepare a specific board (computerized or hand-drawn image) with the answers, plus a few wrong answers, and present the temporary communication board to the participant. If dealing with vision loss, participants can feel/manipulate the object and the number of the object given to them. They can then decide what it may be, based on tactile interpretation (e.g., if using a quarter, an acceptable answer would be "coin" vs. the specific monetary value of the coin).

Cognitive

This program can be used with all levels of cognition. For Alzheimer's participants, use only 2–3 objects, making sure that they are objects with which the participants would be familiar. In the event of word-finding difficulties, participants may draw the answer for themselves/team. Using objects of the same color or size may increase difficulty.

Social/Emotional

Encourage positive support between all group members. This is a great exercise to promote cooperation and peer support. The goal isn't the result but the journey to achieve the result.

Safety Issues

Allow enough time for each team/individual to answer to the best of their ability. Try to mediate the conflict between team members. If the behavior continues, change team members or run the rest of the program in individual format.

Tips and Tricks

- Donated items that you previously thought would have no possible use will come in handy here. Use a book and have participants remember the title. Have volunteers or staff donate trinkets, books, etc.

- Increase the challenge/difficulty by using similar objects (e.g., a coin collection) or items that are all the same color, such as red for Valentine's Day.

- Using soft cloth covers can decrease difficulty—the overall shape of the object can be somewhat determined through the cloth. Boxes make the exercise more challenging. Scrounge from your shipping/ receiving department. Rubber glove boxes work well, or you can use empty tissue boxes. For larger items, consider a cloth covered ice-cream pail.

- Make the medals from juice lids: spray paint them metallic colors, and glue ribbon onto the backs. Ask to have old trophies donated and then, using a piece of foam core board with a handwritten "1st Place" and "2nd Place," hot glue or Velcro the foam core board on over top the existing engraved plaque.

COMMON "SCENTS" TRIVIA CHALLENGE

Objective

To stimulate long-term and short-term memory, to use new information as a learning tool, and to promote long-term memory recall

Targeted Domains and Benefits

Cognitive	problem solving, memory recall, active learning
Social	cooperation, team playing, support for others
Emotional	sense of accomplishment, increased self-esteem and self-confidence

Preparation and Materials

- call ahead to florist for donated flowers
- collect scented oils and cottonballs, if including sensory stimulation activity
- color paper to track scores, if using competitive format
- a pen or pencil per team
- whiteboard/markers or chalkboard/chalk
- fake money in denominations of $50, $100, $500, $1000, $5000, $10,000, $50,000, $100,000 or blank "checks" to write out to the winners (see samples in Appendix)

Procedure

1. Choose whether the group will be participating in teams or as individuals. If using team format, have a group size of four maximum to maintain challenge level.
2. Have teams sit at separate tables (if possible), or in the same general location (group the chairs).
3. Toss a coin to determine which team starts the program. (if playing as individuals, choose from the right or left, as an easy option).
4. Each participant or group is provided with a pen and paper. Write team names on the top of the paper.
5. The facilitator reads the trivia question aloud and provides a predetermined amount (e.g., 30 seconds) of time for each team to answer.

6. Each team will have 30 seconds to discuss the question and 30 seconds to write down their answer. The designated time can be altered to suit participants' processing, verbalization, or writing time and requirements.

7. At the one-minute mark, each team may read their answer aloud to the facilitator, who will then write down each team's answer on the whiteboard/chalkboard.

8. For each correct answer the team/individual receives one point. Tally the points at the game's end, and hand out fake money or fake checks as desired.

Modifications

Physical
This activity works very well for anyone with a physical impairment, as all they need is the ability to verbalize their response to team members or to the facilitator (in individual format). For participants with speaking difficulties, have them scribe the answer for their team, if they are able to write. In the event of having to use a communication board, prepare a specific board (computerized or hand drawn) with the answers, plus a few wrong answers, and present the temporary communication board to the participant.

Cognitive
This program is best used with mid-to-high-range cognitive function. The facilitator can ask questions at their discretion to assure positive success for participants. In the event of an incorrect or nonanswer with lower-functioning participants, have them tell a story related to the answer or flowers in general. This will provide emotional safety (success) for the participants.

Social/Emotional
Encourage positive support between all group members. This is a great exercise to promote a "learn something new every day" approach. The goal isn't the result but the journey to achieve the result.

Safety Issues

Allow enough time for each team/individual to answer to the best of their ability.

Tips and Tricks

- Add visual interest—bring samples of the flowers being described in the program. Ask your local florist to donate "day olds" or fresh flowers (if you are really lucky!) to assist in making your program special. Ask big—ask for enough samples that you will have a flower to give to each participant at the end of the program.

- Bring scented oils that smell like different flowers—this adds a sensory stimulation process into the program and is great for low-functioning participants. Use cotton balls to put the oil on so each participant can have their own sample (this is also good infection control practice).

Flower Trivia

1. What color of rose symbolizes grace?
2. What color of rose says "thank you" and is a sign of admiration?
3. What flower produces the rare spice saffron?
4. What flower bulb can be used to replace an onion in cooking?
5. Egypt's national flower is a water lily of what color?
6. What color of rose implies "desire"?
7. What color of rose represents respect and courage?
8. What is the provincial flower of Alberta?
9. What is the state flower of Alaska?
10. What flower is opium derived from?
11. What color of rose says "I love you"?
12. What is the provincial flower of Saskatchewan?
13. What color of rose is the hardest (almost impossible!) to find?
14. What flower can be used in salad or as tea?
15. What is the state flower of North Dakota?
16. What color of rose signifies spiritual love and purity?
17. What is the provincial flower of Nova Scotia?
18. What flower(s) can be eaten safely?
19. What color of rose symbolizes friendship?
20. What is the provincial flower of Manitoba?
21. What flower is named after an object in space?
22. What flower has a famous cartoon pig named after it?

Answer Key for Flower Trivia

1. Light Pink
2. Dark Pink
3. Crocus
4. Tulip
5. Blue
6. Coral
7. Red
8. Wild Rose
9. Forget-Me-Not
10. Poppy
11. Red
12. Tiger Lily
13. Blue
14. Dandelion
15. Prairie Rose
16. White
17. Mayflower
18. Pansy, Petunia, Dandelion, Tulip
19. Yellow
20. Prairie Crocus
21. Sunflower
22. Petunia

GEOGRAPHIC TRIVIA

Objective

To increase cognitive stimulation and learning through low-level competition and to learn interesting facts about a specific country

Targeted Domains and Benefits

Cognitive	problem solving, memory recall, active learning
Social	cooperation, team playing, support for others
Emotional	sense of accomplishment, increased self-esteem and self-confidence

Preparation and Materials

- a pen or pencil and a piece of paper per team
- a bowl for each participant/team
- jellybeans
- whiteboard/marker or chalkboard/chalk

Procedure

1. Seat participants in groups (if playing as a team) or in a semicircle in front of you, ensuring a clear view of the whiteboard/chalkboard.

2. For either game (Canada or United States), draw four columns on the whiteboard, list the categories at the top of each (i.e., Geography, Provencial/Territorial Capitals, Famous Canadians, Famous Canadian Events), and write the numbers 1–10 along the left side, each followed in parentheses by the corresponding jellybean reward number. The purpose of these whiteboard/chalkboard charts is to keep a running tally of scores and jellybeans won. See an example of scoring in progress in Appendix, page 177.

3. If using the team format, have the teams select a team name.

4. Have one person per team select the question. The team can answer as a whole—each team player gets to choose a question at least once.

5. Have a bowl with the team name in front of it on your front table. A paper folded in half then propped behind the bowl works well. Tip: Make sure you write the name of the team on both sides of the folded paper—that way you always know what bowl(s) to put the jellybeans in!

6. If playing as individuals, small cups work well as jellybean holders. Have players write their names on their cups and hand out the required jellybeans each time they answer a question.

7. Starting on the left, have the team/participant select their question, making sure participants realize that lower numbered questions are generally easier than higher numbered questions. Note: They do not have to start at the top and work their way down—for instance, they can start at number 7, a 10-jellybean question.

8. Read the question out loud and give participants 60 seconds to answer. In the event of a wrong answer, the team/participant receives only one jellybean. Once all the questions in each category have been answered, the game is finished.

Modifications

Physical
Parkinson's/MS/Loss of or reduced vision: Keep all participants/teams "winnings" on the front table and hand them to each individual at the end of the game.

Cognitive
This program is most appropriate for high-functioning participants. In the event of using this program with mid-range cognitive functioning, the facilitator can delete or replace questions to provide for greater group success or provide hints to help the participant/team guess the answer.

Social/Emotional
Be aware of negative group interactions. Small teams of 2–3 work best, as it is easier for the team to come to a consensus.

Safety Issues

Sharing/Teamwork
If at the end of the program there are remaining goodies, ensure that they are split equally among all participants.

Tips and Tricks

- If one team/participant has a small number of jellybeans and appears discouraged, throw in random questions about your facility or activity calendar (ones you are sure that the participant/team will know!) as "bonus bean" questions.

- Recruit a volunteer or family member to research history questions (from many countries) for you and have a whole series of programs dedicated to world learning. Combine this program with video traveling and explore the world together.

Game One: Canada

Category One: Geography (Beans)

1. This province touches the Pacific Ocean. (2)

2. This province boasts a huge iron sculpture of wheat. (4)

3. The Red River Valley is in this province. (5)

4. The North Saskatchewan River originates here. (6)

5. The Great Lakes are part of this province. (7)

6. True or False: Alberta is home to glaciers. (8)

7. Dinosaur remains can be found in this province. (10)

8. This territory was part of the gold rush. (12)

9. "Rupert's Land" refers to this. (14)

10. The Laurentian Mountains are found there. (15)

Category Two: Provincial/Territorial Capitals (Beans)

1. This prairie capital is named after a British Queen. (2)

2. This provincial capital is named after a horse of a specific color. (4)

3. This capital is sometimes referred to as "Winter-peg." (5)

4. The capital city has the same name as its province. (6)

5. This capital city started as a Hudson's Bay trading post. (7)

6. This provincial capital hosts the Canadian Finals Rodeo. (8)

7. This capital city is named after a kitchen tool of a specific color. (10)

8. This capital city is renowned for pewter works. (12)

9. This provincial capital has the world's second largest harbor. (14)

10. This provincial capital was originally called "Frobisher Bay." (15)

Category Three: Famous Canadians (Beans)

1. He was a most eccentric and talented pianist. (2)

2. This cancer patient ran the Marathon of Hope. (4)

3. This most famous hockey player wore number 99. (5)

4. This person invoked the war measures act in 1970. (6)

5. This "First Nations" person was actually British. (7)

6. He instigated the Metîs rebellion in Saskatchewan. (8)

7. She was Canada's first female Governor General. (10)

8. He was the "Father of Medicare." (12)

9. He was the first Prime Minister after Confederation. (14)

10. She is the author of the famous "Anne" books. (15)

Category Four: Famous Canadian Events (Beans)

1. 20% of this city's population died in this explosion. (2)

2. This event caused the "War Measures Act" to be invoked. (4)

3. Paul Henderson scored the winning goal in this famous hockey series. (5)

4. This famous conference was held in PEI in 1864. (6)

5. In 1937 this ship became the official picture on the dime. (7)

6. John McCrae wrote this famous poem in 1915. (8)

7. A tornado hit this prairie city in 1990. (10)

8. In 1951 Hurricane Hazel hit this province. (12)

9. In 1905 Alberta and Saskatchewan did this. (14)

10. This man built Canada's first railway. (15)

Answers to Category One: Geography (Beans)

1. British Columbia (2)

2. Saskatchewan (4)

3. Manitoba (5)

4. Rocky Mountains (6)

5. Ontario (7)

6. True (Columbia Ice Fields) (8)

7. Alberta (10)

8. Yukon (12)

9. The vast land span owned by the Hudson's Bay Co. during the early trading days (14)

10. Quebec (15)

Answers to Category Two: Provincial/Territorial Capitals (Beans)

1. Regina (Saskatchewan) (2)

2. Whitehorse (Yukon Territory) (4)

3. Winnipeg (Manitoba) (5)

4. Quebec City (Quebec) (6)

5. Victoria (British Columbia) (7)

6. Edmonton (Alberta) (8)

7. Yellowknife (N.W.T.) (10)

8. Fredricton (New Brunswick) (12)

9. Halifax (Nova Scotia) (14)

10. Iqaluit (Territory of Nunavut) (15)

Answers to Category Three: Famous Canadians (Beans)

1. Glenn Gould (2)

2. Terry Fox (4)

3. Wayne Gretzky (5)

4. Pierre Elliot Trudeau (6)

5. Grey Owl (Archie Belaney) (7)

6. Louis Riel (8)

7. Jeanne Sauvé (10)

8. Tommy Douglas (12)

9. Sir John A. Macdonald (14)

10. L.M. Montgomery (15)

Answers to Category Four: Famous Canadian Events (Beans)

1. The Halifax Explosion (2)

2. The October Crisis (1970) (4)

3. The Summit Series (5)

4. The Charlottetown Conference (6)

5. The Bluenose (7)

6. In Flander's Field (8)

7. Edmonton (10)

8. Ontario (12)

9. Became provinces (14)

10. John Molson (15)

Game Two: United States

Category One: Geography

1. This state farms the largest amount of land. (2)

2. Fort Knox is located in this state. (4)

3. This state is home to the "Chocolate Capital." (5)

4. The Hoover Dam is found in this state. (6)

5. This state has over 2.7 million acres of forests. (7)

6. Gold was discovered in 1880 in this state. (8)

7. "Devils Tower" is a national monument in this state. (10)

8. An empty lake of salt can be found in this state. (12)

9. This state has 90,000 miles of shoreline. (14)

10. Coffee is grown in this state. (15)

Category Two: State Capitals

1. This state capital has the same name as a sandwich. (2)

2. This state capital is also the name of a saint. (4)

3. This capital can also be used as a man's first name. (5)

4. The capital city's name can indicate fortune or luck. (6)

5. This capital city's name is also that of a famous ship. (7)

6. You might think that witch hunts took place here. (8)

7. There are famous cliffs with the same name. (10)

8. A bit of stone provides the inspiration for this capital. (12)

9. Rhymes with "noisy." (14)

10. This capital city is the first name of a famous president. (15)

Category Three: Famous Americans

1. She was a vaudeville-styled child star. (2)

2. The first African-American to win the Masters (golf). (4)

3. He is known under his pen name "Mark Twain." (5)

4. He was the 3rd president of the United States. (6)

5. He traveled Ohio and Indiana, planting apple orchards. (7)

6. She was both blind and deaf, but learned to speak. (8)

7. She was a native American princess, born in Virginia. (10)

8. A red-headed comedienne with her own television show. (12)

9. A famous baseball player who died of a rare disease called amyotrophic lateral sclerosis, which is now named after him. (14)

10. He illustrated covers for the Saturday Evening Post. (15)

Category Four: Famous American Events

1. What killed 8000 people in Galveston, Texas in 1900? (2)

2. This struck San Francisco on April 18, 1906. (4)

3. He was the first African-American to play baseball. (5)

4. A nuclear accident took place where in 1979? (6)

5. Lincoln's famous speech given in 1863. (7)

6. On January 20, 1961, this president gave his official address. (8)

7. This bridge opened in 1937 and is still one of the longest suspension bridges in the world. (10)

8. Francis Scott Key wrote the words to this song in 1813. (12)

9. In 1851 this law was passed in the state of Maine. (14)

10. Who said, "One small step for man, one giant leap for mankind?" (15)

Answers to Category One: Geography (Beans)

1. Texas (2)

2. Kentucky (4)

3. Pennsylvania (Hershey) (5)

4. Nevada (6)

5. Maryland (7)

6. Alaska (8)

7. Wyoming (10)

8. Utah (12)

9. Minnesota (more than California, Florida, and Hawaii combined!) (14)

10. Hawaii (15)

Answers to Category Two: State Capitals (Beans)

1. Denver (Colorado) (2)

2. Helena (Montana) (4)

3. Montgomery (Alabama) (5)

4. Providence (Rhode Island) (6)

5. Bismarck (North Dakota) (7)

6. Salem (Oregon) (8)

7. Dover (Delaware) (10)

8. Little Rock (Arkansas) (12)

9. Boise (Idaho) (14)

10. Lincoln (Nebraska) (15)

Answers to Category Three: Famous Americans (Beans)

1. Shirley Temple (2)

2. Tiger Woods (4)

3. Samuel Clemens (5)

4. Thomas Jefferson (6)

5. Johnny "Appleseed" Chapman (7)

6. Helen Keller (8)

7. Pocahontas (10)

8. Lucille Ball (12)

9. Lou Gherig (14)

10. Norman Rockwell (15)

Answers to Category Four: Famous American Events (Beans)

1. Hurricane (2)

2. Earthquake (4)

3. Jackie Robinson (5)

4. Three Mile Island (Pennsylvania) (6)

5. The Gettysburg Address (7)

6. John F. Kennedy (8)

7. The Golden Gate Bridge (10)

8. The Star Spangled Banner (12)

9. Law of Prohibition (14)

10. Neil Armstrong (1969) (15)

Section 2

Active Games

It's time to get busy! These fun formats will turn work into fun. With only a few basic supplies like beanbags, pool noodles, balloons, and dice you can create hours of fun and enjoyment. There are special event games (you know, those games that take that extra work and manpower) as well as games for everyday use.

These games have been designed to play while seated but can always be transformed into a moving and grooving active game by combining different levels of physical functioning. A clinical benefit to these exercises is that an assessment team has a great opportunity to observe and assess by sitting in on your group.

Just remember—if it looks like you are enjoying yourself and having fun, your group will pick up on that enthusiasm. So let's get busy batting around balloons, doing chair exercises, and playing wild and wacky dice games!

POOL NOODLE HOCKEY

Objective

To provide recreational exercise in a noncompetitive environment, to improve ROM and potentially increase nutrition/hydration of participants

Targeted Domains and Benefits

Physical	hand–eye coordination, bending, reaching, grasping
Social	sharing equipment, peer support, cooperation
Emotional	increased feelings of success, pleasure in "winning"

Preparation and Materials

- set up chairs in circle formation (8 maximum), the width of the pool noodle apart
- if using a group larger than eight, set up two rows of chairs facing each other
- use chairs with arms to decrease risk of falls!
- a pool noodle (cut a regular length noodle in half) per person
- an arm chair per person
- balloons to share

Procedure

1. Blow up 1–2 balloons (use different colors if using more than one balloon).
2. Set up participants in a circular formation (noncompetitive) or single file (two rows facing each other for low level competition).
3. Provide each participant with a foam noodle.
4. Create a scenario for the game (e.g., Stanley Cup Final).
5. The object of the game is to keep the balloon off the floor as much as possible. Remind participants to avoid hitting others with the noodle while playing. Reduce this risk by seating participants a noodle-width apart.

6. The facilitator/volunteers keep the balloon "in play" (off the floor). When the balloon floats out of noodle range, they pick up the balloon and bat it back into the circle (or in between the rows).

7. Encourage participants to hit the balloon as it comes their direction, and to support other players by batting the balloon toward them.

8. This game allows for both noncompetitive and low-level competitive action. Higher functioning participants can choose which option they prefer and select their teams accordingly.

9. If playing in teams, determine accrual of points by a) which team let the balloon hit the floor (when in circular formation) or b) which team hit it behind the opposition (when in single row formation).

Modifications

Physical
Parkinson's/MS/Loss of or reduced vision: Tensor-wrap the participant's hand to the noodle to alleviate dropping/throwing of pool noodle. The facilitator/volunteers buddies-up with the visually impaired participant to provide verbal cueing.

Safety Issues

Negative Social Behavior
Do not allow participants to hit others with noodles. Even if action is inferred, immediately utilize behavior modification. If the behavior persists, remove the noodle from the participant and create a new role for them (i.e., referee/balloon tosser).

Tips and Tricks

- Cutting each pool noodle in half creates twice as many noodles, and the length is a safe length to operate for most participants.
- Use your imagination...it's a seventh game Stanley Cup Final, it's a "pond-hockey" tournament—your energy is what the participants will feed off of, so go wild!

BIG DICE GAMES

Objective

To provide a mild to moderate level of cognitive and physical stimulation through the use of gross motor skills and addition/sequencing skills

Targeted Domains and Benefits

Physical   hand–eye coordination, bending, reaching, grasping, tactile stimulation

Social   sharing equipment, peer support

Cognitive   mental math skills, following sequential directions

Preparation and Materials

- set up chairs in a semi-circle with a large, open area in front of the chairs
- an arm chair per person
- a pen or pencil per person
- big dice
- format sheets
- whiteboard and marker or chalkboard/chalk
- deck of cards

Procedure

1. Decide which format you will use for this session. If playing with more than five participants, divide players into teams of five with each team taking a turn using the dice.
2. Following the format sheets, continue until the selected game is completed. In the event of finishing early, select another format sheet and continue playing until the program time is up.

Modifications

Physical

Hemiplegia/Quadraplegia/reduced vision: For participants unable to throw, place the dice on the edge of a table/counter and have them push the dice off the edge. Quadriplegia can be addressed by having that participant select a "pinch-hitter" or by having them assist in making sure the format is followed. Another option is to place the dice on participants' heads and have them move their heads backward to "roll" the dice to the floor behind them (be careful that no edges come in contact with facial areas).

Emotional
Provide encouragement and/or assistance as required to reduce the risk of frustration and failure for participants.

Safety Issues

Physical Safety
When seating participants, ensure that no one is in the direct path of a potential dice throw.

Tips and Tricks

- Find old car seat covers at a second hand store as a cheaper alternative to fake-fur.
- Ask for fabric donations—check to see if your local fabric store will donate roll-ends or provide them to you at minimal cost.
- Use big pieces of packing newsprint for a cost-effective way to post the group format on the wall—it's cheaper than buying a flip chart! You can find it in most delivery boxes.

Format One—Dice Bingo

Post two large pieces of paper on the wall (or use a whiteboard/chalkboard if available) and draw a grid that results in nine spaces (make a six-space grid when using with an Alzheimer's group) for each team.

Using a deck of cards, draw nine or six cards for each team and mark the card value in an open space as each card is drawn. Aces are low, Jack is 11, Queen is 12, and King is 13. Once bingo cards are created, have each team collectively roll their five dice.

Using the numbers they rolled, the team chooses which square they would like to block off (mark as completed). They can choose any combination in order to complete a square (e.g., to block off a Queen, any combination of the dice totaling 12 can be used).

After the team makes its selection, put a Post-it note over the square they have chosen to give the team a visual guide for which squares/numbers still remain to be rolled. Repeat this procedure with the second team and continue until all squares have been blocked off.

Format Two—Dice Rummy

Post the sequence list on large paper or whiteboard to assist with visual cueing. There are two blank spots to write in your own combinations.

Each team of 5 will roll their dice (one for each team member) and, with each turn, work their way down the sequence sheet. If a team is not successful in rolling their assigned sequence in one team roll (a total of five dice throws) they must re-do that step on their next turn. Only once a step has been successfully rolled can they move to the next step (i.e., within five rolls, the team must roll two "ones" to move to the next sequence on their next turn). Begin with one team rolling and then alternate between teams, continuing in this fashion until one team finishes their sequential list first.

Sequence Sheet

SEQUENCE	TEAM ONE	TEAM TWO
2 - Ones		
2 - Fours		
2 - Sixes		
1 - One, 1 - Two, 1 - Three		
2 - Fours, 2 - Sixes		
1 - Five, 1 - Three, 1 - One		
1 - Four, 2 - Twos		
2 - Threes, 1 - Six		

DONUT ON A STRING

Objective

To provide a mild to moderate level of physical activation involving range of motion and motor coordination.

Targeted Domains and Benefits

Physical	upper body coordination, bending, tactile stimulation
Social	peer support and encouragement, patience
Cognitive	strategy/decision-making skills, kinesthetic awareness

Preparation and Materials

- hang a string from a high area (i.e., balcony railing, shower rod)
- an arm chair per person
- a string and donut per person
- a napkin per person
- scissors
- latex gloves
- shower rod

Procedure

1. Cut each participant a length of string that will allow the donuts to hang at mouth level while participants are seated. Wearing latex gloves, tie these portions of string around the donut and then knot the donut/string section to the long pieces knotted from the higher support.

2. If using a shower rod, place the rod in a doorway and have a volunteer hold the rod while participants are playing. If using a doorway, participants will need to take single turns. Ensure that single participants are placed facing the remainder of the group to allow for cheering and encouragement.

3. At the count of three, have each participant attempt to chew their donut off the string using only their mouth and trunk movement (no hands!) The first person to chew their donut off the string wins.

4. Provide a napkin for participants to wipe down faces (napkins can also be used to tuck in front of shirt to keep clothes clean).

Modifications

Physical
Reduced vision/Parkinson's: Provide verbal cueing for visual impairment. Adjust donut height, or simply hold the donut on the string versus tying it to a support if Parkinson's tremors are severe.

Emotional
Lead by example—motivate other participants in cheering and helpful suggestions.

Safety Issues

Physical Safety
It is vital that you know your participants' dietary restrictions. Be aware of any diabetic issues. Be aware of and watch for any signs of choking. Encourage small bites, which is easier to do if you use smaller donuts versus regular-sized donuts.

Tips and Tricks

- This is a great game to use at group socials and family/participant special events (it works especially well at Halloween).
- Assign nursing staff designates to help run the program to have them close at hand in the event of an emergency. I have never encountered any choking issues when using this program but always be proactive in reducing risks!

PYRAMID TOSS

Objective

To provide a mild to moderate level of physical activation and cognitive stimulation

Targeted Domains and Benefits

Physical   hand–eye coordination, bending, reaching, grasping, throwing

Social   peer support/encouragement

Cognitive   picture recognition

Preparation and Materials

- take staff photos with a digital camera
- an arm chair per person
- beanbags
- picture boxes

Procedure PRIOR TO Session

1. To make the pyramid, use hollow, lightweight cardboard boxes. Check with your local bakery—8" or 12" cake boxes make the perfect target!

2. Place some rice inside the boxes (enough to make noise) and use clear parcel tape to securely tape all edges, sealing in the rice and reinforcing the box's stability.

3. Once boxes are sealed, attach selected artwork/picture to one or more sides of the box. Use clipart, magazine pictures, calendar pictures, letters, shapes, colors—anything that will encourage participants to recognize and distinguish the difference between the boxes.

Procedure

1. Set up nine picture boxes, with all the pictures facing toward the participants, on a table in a pyramid shape.

2. Seat participants in a semicircle with the center chair in the semicircle (the "player chair") closest to the pyramid.

3. Move participants into the player chair when it is their turn to toss.

4. Give each participant in the player chair 3 beanbags—they will get three turns.

5. The facilitator decides what picture they want the participant to aim for, or simply gives the participant the goal of knocking all the boxes off the table.

Modifications

Physical

Reduced vision/Parkinson's: Provide verbal cueing for visual impairment. For all physical restrictions, simply move participants closer to boxes to ensure success.

Cognitive

Alzheimer's: Put three boxes with all different pictures on table. Select which one the participant should aim at.

Safety Issues

Physical Safety

Ensure that no person is within the throwing range of the participants, or close enough to be hit by falling boxes.

Tips and Tricks

- Check with shoe stores to see if you can get empty shoeboxes— they work nicely as well. Try to get white ones, as it makes seeing the pictures that much easier.

- If increasing ROM is a target goal, set the boxes at different heights using ice cream pails and other materials to place the boxes on and alter the distance the participant must throw the beanbag. Turn the participants backward and make them toss it over their heads!

HUMAN BOWLING

Objective

To provide a mild to moderate level of physical activation and cognitive stimulation

Targeted Domains and Benefits

Physical   hand–eye coordination, bending, reaching, grasping, throwing

Social   peer support and encouragement

Cognitive   color recognition, staff recall

Preparation and Materials

- 6 aprons (each a different color)
- an arm chair per person
- beach ball

Procedure

1. Recruit six staff members and have each of them wear a unique color apron. Instruct participants to aim from the chest down, preferably the lower leg/foot area.
2. Have staff members line up as follows: three in front, two in middle, one at back. Place each participant a minimum five feet in front of the human bowling pins. When the beach ball hits a human pin, that person theatrically falls to the ground. Give each participant three turns with the beach ball to knock down all the human pins.

Modifications

Physical
MS/Hemiplegia/Stroke/Cerebral Palsy/Reduced Vision: Provide verbal cueing for visual impairment. For all physical restrictions: move the participants closer to human pins. The facilitator can hold the beach ball in front of the participants and have them push/punch or kick the beach ball toward the human pins.

Cognitive
Alzheimer's: Direct participants to hit a certain color.

Emotional
Encourage the human pins to be dramatic when "falling," as it induces more laughter and focused action in the participants.

Safety Issues

Physical Safety
Ensure that the beach ball is soft enough to not cause injury to the human pins. Redirect the participants' aim as necessary.

Tips and Tricks

- Have the human pins bring aprons from home. It makes for much laughter when the male human pins are wearing frilly type aprons, and you save money!
- Get old, printed drapes or sheets from a second hand store and cut out rectangles with long ties on two sides. This is an inexpensive way to make aprons.

BEAN BAG SHUFFLEBOARD

Objective

To provide a mild to moderate level of physical activation and cognitive stimulation

Targeted Domains and Benefits

Physical   hand–eye coordination, bending, reaching, grasping, throwing

Social   peer support/encouragement

Cognitive   number recognition, mental math, sequencing skills

Preparation and Materials

- clear out/rearrange furniture in program area if necessary
- an arm chair per person
- beanbags
- masking tape
- letter-size paper

Procedure prior to session

1. Prepare your game area. You can use any shape you like, but a rectangle 60 inches long by 30 inches wide is suggested. Follow the diagram provided to tape out boundaries.
2. Inside of each boundary, tape down a piece of paper with the value written on it in large print.

Procedure

1. Decide, either as the facilitator or by group consensus, the grand total everyone will be aiming for. Seat each participant a minimum of five feet behind the bottom of the rectangle.
2. Each participant has three beanbags to toss onto the board, and the total of all three tosses will be that turn's score. Continue until all participants have reached their final required total.

Modifications

Physical
MS/Hemiplegia/Stroke/Cerebral Palsy/Reduced Vision: Provide verbal cueing for visual impairment. For all physical restrictions: Move participants closer to floorboard. Place severely impaired participants at the bottom of the circle and have them push the beanbags with a pool noodle (if using this method, have the group agree that these participants will receive double point value for their pushes).

Cognitive
Alzheimer's: Direct participants to hit a certain color of paper (write the points on various colored sheets of paper).

Social
Encourage peer support by assigning "cheerleading" moves (e.g., arm movements, chants) to the waiting participants.

Safety Issues

Social Concerns
Ensure that participants are successful in achieving a point value for each of their tosses.

Tips and Tricks

- Make up silly rules on the fly if you see participants encountering difficulty with their tosses (e.g., if the beanbag lands outside the rectangle or if you squawk like a chicken, it's two bonus points!).

- Use garbage cans with point values taped to the outside to change the format and keep it fresh. This also makes it easier to adjust the distance with the cans versus moving people around.

30	50	30
25		20
10		15
	5	

FRONTIER EXERCISES

Objective

To provide a mild to moderate level of physical activation and cognitive stimulation

Targeted Domains and Benefits

Physical   hand–eye coordination, bending, reaching, grasping, throwing

Cognitive   following visual/verbal cueing, sequencing, timing

Preparation and Materials

* an arm chair per person
* music/stereo

Procedure

1. Seat participants in a semicircle facing the facilitator. Ensure that the stereo/music is within reach of the facilitator. Do a test-run of volume—play a bit of the selection and talk over it to ensure that all participants can hear the instructions clearly.

2. Provide overall directions for the session: a) only do as much as they are comfortable doing, b) keep backs straight, and c) remember to breathe! Start the warm up without music, using the following steps:

   * *Hand clenches*: Open/close fists, clenching when in fist position, stretching hand out completely in open position.

   * *Arm raises*: One arm at a time, reach straight above the head, stretching for the ceiling.

   * *Knee raises*: One leg at a time, keep knee bent and raise knee toward chest. Ensure that all participants maintain a straight back during this exercise.

   * *Trunk rotation*: Crossing arms over chest, rotate slowly from the center to the left, then return to center. Repeat four times to both left and right directions.

- *Neck stretches*: Slowly bend the neck sideways, reaching with the ear toward the left shoulder. Slowly return to center and repeat on the right side. Repeat four times per side.

- *Ankle rotations*: Extend lower leg so foot is off the floor. Slowly rotate each ankle 360° in both clockwise and counter-clockwise directions. Repeat twice for each ankle.

3. Using simple 4-count music (big band music works very well) use the following sequence—introduce each action with the title so participants can anticipate movements:

   - *Getting water from the well*: Raise right hand to center above the head. At top of the stretch, clench the fist as if grasping a rope. Pull down (still clenched) to lap and release. Repeat with left hand. Repeat eight times.

   - *Vacuuming*: Place clenched fists one in front of the other, as if grasping a tube. Keep back straight, extend arms fully, and bend from the hips, extending to a left diagonal. Return to center and extend in same position to front center. Return to center and extend in same position to a right diagonal. Repeat eight times.

   - *Mopping the floor*: Make fists and place on top of each other, as if grasping a mop handle. Starting from center, rotate trunk to the left, then all the way to the right, then back to center, keeping the back straight. Repeat eight times.

   - *Baking bread*: Start with fists in lap. Using a forward shoulder rotation, bring right fist up, back, and around and then back into lap, as if punching down bread dough. Repeat action with left fist. Repeat eight times.

   - *Flying*: Arms down by sides, fingers pointing to the floor. Raise arms simultaneously to shoulder height. At top of movement (shoulder height), flex wrists so that fingers are pointing up. Lower to starting position. Repeat eight times.

   - *Tiptoes*: Place hands flat on each knee. Raise each foot onto the toes, to beat of music, one at a time, and then return heel to the floor. Repeat eight times for each foot.

   - *Saturday dance*: With hands flat on each knee and to beat of music, raise toes off floor and back again. Repeat eight times for each foot.

- ***Kick the can***: Keeping back straight, extend one leg at a time, raising the lower leg to a 45° angle. Important—do not completely extend the leg and lock the knee! Repeat eight times for each foot.

- ***Squashing grasshoppers***: With a straight back and knee in a 90° position, raise knee towards chest, keeping foot flat. Bring knee back down, making sure the complete sole of the foot meets the floor. Repeat eight times for each knee.

4. For cool down, repeat warm up process, in a slow, relaxing manner.

5. When the program is completed, ensure that each participant drinks fluids prior to leaving and check on physical status (e.g., sore, hurting, comfortable).

Modifications

Physical
MS/Hemiplegia/Stroke/Cerebral Palsy/Reduced Vision: Provide verbal cueing for visual impairment. For all physical restrictions, have participants follow the movements they are able to follow. Have adaptations (e.g. knee raises) ready. If a participant experiences difficulties with hip movement, reduce lifting height, or have them repeat the foot lifts instead of the knee lifts.

Cognitive
Alzheimer's: Do not use music with Alzheimer's participants. Use physical cueing and energetic directions to stimulate participation instead.

Safety Issues

Physical Concerns
Know participants' relevant physical ability (e.g., have they had recent hip surgery?). If necessary, have the participants' obtain a physician's letter allowing them to participate.

Tips and Tricks

- Try not to wear dark pants—lighter colored pants make it easier for participants to visually track what you are doing.

- Ask family members to bring in favorite CD's of their loved ones to help keep the class fresh.

PARACHUTE GAMES

Objective

To provide a mild to moderate level of physical activation and cognitive stimulation

Targeted Domains and Benefits

Physical	hand–eye coordination, bending, reaching, grasping, ROM
Social	peer support/encouragement, teamwork
Cognitive	visual/auditory recognition, following directions

Preparation and Materials

- an arm chair per person
- parachute
- 3 soft balls—beach balls or Nerf balls work well

Procedure

1. Seat participants in a circle with a parachute handhold in front of each of them.
2. Have participants practice waving the parachute up and down at the same time (making a mushroom) and also with each participant waving it at different times (creating a wave). Explain each term you use (mushroom, wave) as they are practicing.
3. Explain that when you yell out "Popcorn" they need to wave as hard as they can. When you yell "Mushroom," they must use the movements to create the mushroom.
4. As participants create a wave pattern, toss one ball onto the parachute. After a few moments, yell out "Popcorn!" and create a waving frenzy. Decrease the frenzy by yelling "Mushroom!"
5. Repeat with the rest of the balls, until all three balls are popcorning on the parachute at the same time.
6. When using the "mushroom," the facilitator can quickly walk under the parachute while it is in this phase. Give the participants an option to "trap" you on these walks by using teamwork to quickly

pull the parachute out of the mushroom and down toward the floor in order to trap you underneath.

7. Another option is to have the facilitator and a volunteer gently toss a ball across the parachute to each other. The participants must work as a team to use the mushroom to block the toss.

Modifications

Physical
MS/Hemiplegia/Stroke/Cerebral Palsy/Reduced Vision: Provide verbal cueing for visual impairment. For limb restriction, have participants use their strong side when grasping the parachute. For those with weak tone or with involuntary movements, ensure that the waving motion does not become so frantic as to cause overextension of the arms, which could create soreness and stiffness in the participant, or that the parachute handhold does not become entangled too far up the limb.

Cognitive
Alzheimer's: Use one ball at a time. Have the facilitator run under the parachute while participants wave it.

Safety Issues

Physical
Ensure that participants with physical challenges do not get wrapped up, or slip into, the parachute handholds. Watch for balls landing in participants' facial area.

Tips and Tricks

- Make your own parachute! Purchase an old sheet from a second-hand store. It is optional to use it as is, or cut it into a circle. For coloring, use as is or consider tie dying. Cut out as many hand-holds as you need and double stitch around the openings. Serge around the outside of the sheet, and it is ready to use.
- Use balloons with some rice in them instead of beach balls or Nerf-balls.
- This programs works very well in an intergenerational setting—assign a child to partner with one of your participants. Have the children run underneath, while the participants try to "trap" the children.

BEAN BAG STORY TOSS

Objective

To provide a mild to moderate level of physical activation and cognitive stimulation

Targeted Domains and Benefits

Physical	hand–eye coordination, bending, reaching, grasping, ROM
Social	peer support/encouragement
Cognitive	listening skills, kinesthetic awareness

Preparation and Materials

- an arm chair per person
- bean bags
- story

Procedure

1. Seat participants in a circle. Have each participant hold a beanbag.
2. The story provided at the end of this plan has the directional movement in capitals. As the facilitator reads the story, the participants toss/pass the beanbags in the direction that is read as part of the story. There are three directions: right, left, keep.
3. Provide the group with an example prior to starting: "The boy knew he had done the RIGHT thing," at which point all participants pass their bean bags to the person on the right.

Modifications

Physical

Stroke/CP/Reduced Vision: Instruct participants on each side of the visually impaired participant to place the beanbag in or on that participant's hand. For limb restriction, have participants' use their strong side to pass the beanbag, or to increase function, have them try to use their weak side for a portion of the game. For those with weak tone or with involuntary movements, seat them closer to the facilitator to assist as necessary. Provide sufficient time for passing to occur before restarting the story.

Cognitive
Alzheimer's: Simplify the story or simply use the directional words to have participants move the beanbags around the group.

Social
Encourage each participant to verbally support the other players.

Safety Issues

Physical
Behavior issues: Create an alternate role for that participant (e.g., have them act as your assistant and read portions of the story).

Tips and Tricks

- Provide a volunteer with a sample story and then have them write a few more. Stories that make participants laugh at the same time are always a big hit. This would be a great project for a school (elementary to college) English class to take on! Afterward the students can come and play their "game" with your participants as an intergenerational exercise.

Story

Jane was tired of the jungle. Tarzan had LEFT on another safari and LEFT her behind again. She stared around their jungle shack in dismay, knowing it would serve him RIGHT if she starched his loincloth, but she knew she would never do that. After all, he did KEEP his promises, even if he LEFT her stranded for days with no company other than the monkeys.

Jane decided that she had better make things RIGHT and a good way to start was by cleaning up the dishes LEFT from yesterday. It was a good plan, but all that did was get Jane all riled up again about being LEFT behind to clean the banana shack. Jane knew she was RIGHT, but somehow she always LEFT that discussion in the background when Tarzan sailed in on his vine to sweep her into his RIGHT arm to KEEP her entertained before he LEFT again on some other jungle mission. Suddenly, Jane heard a noise to the RIGHT of the banana tree. She wasn't too worried—Tarzan had only LEFT minutes ago and he probably forgot something again. Jane began to worry when she didn't hear Tarzan KEEP to his regular routine of whistling out on the deck. It had to be the poachers—perhaps coming to kidnap her and KEEP her for ransom. Jane was sure she was RIGHT—she had to stop the poachers—she had to save the monkeys and the banana shack! Tarzan always LEFT his bamboo toothpicks by the sundial. Jane slunk to the RIGHT and there were only two toothpicks LEFT! Grabbing one toothpick, she snuck behind the kitchen door (which Tarzan had LEFT open…again!) and waited. Suddenly, there was Tarzan—Jane screamed like the monkeys and leapt from behind the door meaning to make things RIGHT, but Tarzan tripped on the loincloth Jane had LEFT on the floor and fell onto his RIGHT arm.

Tarzan yelled, Jane screamed, and the loincloth shriveled. After much confusion, Jane LEFT the toothpicks on the table, Tarzan made sure she was all RIGHT, and made her swear to KEEP all his loincloths off the floor in the future. Jane smiled—she was always RIGHT.

FRISBEE LIMBO

Objective

To provide a mild to moderate level of physical activation and cognitive stimulation

Targeted Domains and Benefits

Physical   hand–eye coordination, bending, reaching, grasping, ROM

Social   peer support/encouragement

Preparation and Materials

- an arm chair per person
- Frisbee
- limbo stick

Procedure

1. Seat participants in a line facing the limbo stick area.
2. The facilitator holds the limbo stick at varying heights while participants attempt to throw their Frisbee over the limbo stick. With each successful Frisbee throw, the limbo stick moves higher from the ground.
3. Each participant gets one or two turns (at the facilitator's discretion) to throw the Frisbee over level one (again, the height is at the facilitator's discretion). Each participant throws at the same height.
4. When all participants have completed level one, the Frisbee returns to the first participant, the facilitator moves the limbo stick to the second level, and each participant goes again.
5. Participants can continue taking turns until time is up, or the facilitator can choose to eliminate the participants who miss (starting on the second or third turn so that each participant is ensured at least two turns), and continue to eliminate them until only one participant remains.
6. Use half-sized pool noodles as javelins instead of a Frisbee, if so desired.

Modifications

Physical

Stroke/Cerebral Palsy/Reduced Vision: Facilitators can provide visual cueing as necessary. For limb restriction, have participants use their strong side to pass throw the Frisbee. To increase function, have participants try to use their weak side for a portion of the game. For those with weak tone, or involuntary movements, move limbo stick closer to the participant to assist as necessary, or change the Frisbee to a balloon.

Safety Issues

Physical: Use a "Floating Frisbee" (the soft ones) to avoid having it hit another participant.

Tips and Tricks

- Have any volunteers, and yourself, dress up in tropical costume (a coconut bra always makes people laugh).
- Adopt a fake island accent during your instructions.
- A cane works very well for a limbo stick, or you can use a pool noodle or an old straw broom.

Section 3
Tasty Treats

Just like the name suggests, these recipes are delicious! Suggested materials are provided, but you will still need to have on hand a basic baking set. This should include the following items:

- Set of three mixing bowls
- Knife block (with knives!)
- Electric mixer
- Medium-sized roaster pan
- Kitchen linen: oven mitts, dishtowels, dishcloths, aprons
- Two of each utensil: spatula, wooden spoon, slotted spoon, measuring cups, measuring spoons, cutting board
- Two of each baking tray (nonstick is best): cookie tray, 8" square cake pan, 9x13 cake pan, 9" round cake pan, muffin tray, loaf pan, wire cooling racks
- One each—soup ladle, gravy ladle, flat flipping spatula

Many of these items can be donated by family members and/or staff if you put them on a wish list. Taking care of a basic baking set will help the set to last for years before replacement. These recipes call for mostly "by hand" work—I hardly ever use an electric mixer; it loses half the work value that way.

Quick-Mix Breakfast

Objective

To create a nutritional premixed breakfast with quick preparation time

Targeted Domains and Benefits

Physical	hand–eye coordination, manual dexterity, ROM, muscle tone
Social	sharing equipment, general conversation, peer support
Cognitive	sequential processing, measuring
Emotional	feelings of pleasure and joy in creating a personally crafted gift

Preparation and Materials

- photocopy recipe (as large as possible)
- confirm microwave works
- confirm participants have no allergies to proposed ingredients
- pint jars with lids
- small microwaveable container/bowl
- spoons
- aprons
- ingredients
- wet/dry cloths (for clean up)

Procedure

1. Divide participants into pairs. Allot each pair a prearranged area of the table (necessary materials already at places). Review recipe as a group.

2. Allow sufficient time for participants to complete the dry mix (can double recipe, or repeat two times). Once finished, fill 1 pint-jar per person with dry mix. There will be approximately 1/2 cup per individual left over. This portion will be used for the taste test.

3. Have participants decide what they would like to use as their wet ingredient: milk or water. Have each group place their quick-mix into the microwave and, following timing directions, complete the cooking process.

4. Upon completion, reseat each group at the table and begin eating. While participants are eating, discuss the recipe and reminisce about cooking experiences (e.g., What do you remember eating for breakfast when you were little? What was your favorite breakfast? What was your worst breakfast? Did you ever cook breakfast on a wood stove?).

Modifications

Physical

Parkinson's/MS/Loss of or reduced vision/Apraxia/Aphasia: Provide a large print recipe and read the recipe aloud as the group moves through the activity. Create signals—nodding for yes or no. Bring along a pad of paper and a large pen so participants can write what they are trying to say. Also, if the participant is new to the group, the facilitator may want to join that specific group (be the 3rd member).

Cognitive

This program can be used with any cognitive functioning level. For Alzheimer's participants, use simple one-step instructions and physical cueing as necessary.

Safety Issues

Pint Jars

Make sure that jars are not cracked or chipped in any way to avoid cuts!

First Aid/Clean Up

Have Band-Aids readily available to attend to any little cuts. Have a broom/dustpan available in the event that a jar is dropped.

Extension Cords

Make sure extension cords are either completely out of the walking path or range of motion of every participant, or taped down if this option is not available.

Aprons

Provide aprons to protect clothes from cooking supplies (cloth ones are most appropriate).

Tips and Tricks

- Ask family members to donate a portion of the required dry goods or to provide a pint-jar for their family member. Ask them to volunteer to assist in the program as well—volunteering can provide the family member with a greater sense of ownership (and this helps to build support for other programs!), as well as an opportunity to spend time with their loved one.

- Put out a general call for mason jars—there's always someone who has a box they would love to get rid of. This may entail having to purchase new rubber rings, but any donation is better than none!

- Scour garage sales—they're great places to find glass jars (but watch for chips/cracks!)

- Contact your local thrift store to see if they will donate "x" number of jars for your program.

Quick-Mix Breakfast Recipe

3 cups	rolled oats (quick oats)
1 cup	dried fruit
1/8 cup	sesame seeds
1/8 cup	flax seeds (can substitute raisins)
1/2 tbsp	cinnamon
1 pinch	salt
3/4 cup	milk or water

Directions

1. Mix all dry ingredients together.
2. Put 1/2 cup dry mix in a bowl and add a pinch of salt.
3. Add 3/4 cup milk or water to dry mix. Stir.
4. Microwave on high for one minute. Stir.
5. Microwave again on high for 45 seconds.
6. Take out of microwave and let stand for 30 seconds to thicken.

Note: This recipe will provide enough for two pint jars.

SENSATIONAL SUMMER SMOOTHIES

Objective

Create a summertime treat for all fluid-level types and to add nutritional value

Targeted Domains and Benefits

Physical	hand–eye coordination, manual dexterity, ROM, muscle tone
Social	sharing equipment, general conversation, peer support
Cognitive	sequential processing, decision-making
Emotional	sense of purpose, satisfaction in completion

Preparation and Materials

- decorate program area as appropriate for selected theme
- photocopy recipe (as large as possible)
- confirm blender works
- confirm participants have no allergies to proposed ingredients
- ingredients
- plastic (clear) cups
- flexi-straws
- dishcloths/dishtowels
- aprons

Procedure

1. There are two implementation methods: Either the facilitator makes smoothies for participants (large group), or the residents make smoothies for themselves/each other (individual). Depending on which format is selected, the facilitator may have the participants prepare the fruit at the beginning of the program. They can twist greens off strawberries, cut bananas in half, peel peaches, etc.

2. Large Group Format: Have all required materials on the activity table (e.g., have the fruit on plates so participants can see/smell the fruit). Seat participants in small groups around the activity

table, ensuring each participant can see the activity table clearly. Use "restaurant waiter" style interaction to take orders and make each participant's order under their watchful eyes. Call out the ingredients as they are added into the blender. In large-group format, the facilitator can usually make enough in one blender turn to produce two smoothies. Pour smoothies immediately after blending.

3. Individual Format: This one is best used with a small group. Have all materials on the activity table (e.g., have fruit on plates so participants can see/smell the fruit) and seat participants around the activity table. Hint: If using a very large table, the blender can usually be slid in front of each participant if you have enough cord. Have each participant select which fruit they would like (or not!), and also have them measure out or peel (e.g., bananas) fruit as required. Have participants place each ingredient into the blender, and then blend their smoothie. Pour smoothie immediately after blending.

Modifications

Physical
Decreased fine/gross motor skills, decreased vision: Assist participants to the degree they are comfortable. Create the opportunity for participants to make decisions (cognition), rather than asking for physical participation. An added benefit of this program is the enhanced nutritional intake of participants. Add Ensure along with/instead of milk to provide increased nutritional intake for participants experiencing weight loss and/or decreased appetites.

Cognitive
This program can be used with any cognitive functioning level. If using with Alzheimer's participants, use colorful ice cream (or food coloring) and simply have them select a fruit they enjoy.

Social
If a participant exhibits low social mannerisms/problematic behaviors, use the opportunity to sit 1:1 with the participant and quietly partner with him or her to promote acceptable social behaviors.

Safety Issues

Dietary Issues
It is very important to know each participant's allergy alert(s) and fluid-level (thickness) prior to participation.

Extension Cords
Make sure extension cords are either completely out of the walking path
or range of motion of every participant, or taped down if this option is not
available.

Aprons
Provide aprons to protect clothes from cooking supplies (cloth ones are most
appropriate).

Tips and Tricks

- If trying to accommodate a special holiday/occasion, use food-
  coloring to color vanilla ice-cream (e.g., for Remembrance Day,
  use flag colors in layers in a clear plastic cup). For multiple colors,
  it is best to use the same number of blenders as colors!

- Pour leftover smoothie mix, into frozen-pop molds and freeze to
  make "smoothie bars" to use as a special treat in following days.

- This is a great way to take your participants on a Tropical
  Holiday—whether you create the atmosphere on a nice sunny day
  with beach music and a limbo contest or choose to do it in the
  midst of winter in a tropical-holiday decorated room.

- It is also a great fundraiser. Have high-functioning participants
  assist you with a 'Smoothie Sensations" table and sell smoothies
  to raise funds for your program. My smoothies sell for $3.00/cup
  (plastic beer cups), and most of the ice cream (and most fruit) is
  donated. As a result, the program fund grows!

Sensational Smoothies

2 1/2 cups	ice cream
3/4 cup	milk
1/4 cup	Ensure (optional; if not using, add 1/2 cup more ice cream)
1/2 cup	fruit
4 drops	food coloring (optional)

Directions

1. Add ingredients in order listed above.
2. Blend until smooth (depending on fruit selected, smoothie may be
   a little bumpy even when blending is completed).
3. Pour immediately into glasses and serve.

Note: This recipe makes two smoothies.

TRADITIONAL SUNDAY DINNER

Objective

Use tactile stimulation (smell/taste) to stimulate both long- and short-term memory use

Targeted Domains and Benefits

Physical	hand–eye coordination, fine motor skills
Social	general conversation, reinforcing social behaviors
Cognitive	reminiscing, sensory stimulation
Emotional	creating a family-style gathering, fostering emotional growth of group

Preparation and Materials

- decorate eating area as a "home-styled" kitchen (tablecloths, pretty napkins, matching dinnerware—not plastic!)
- a place setting per participant—plate, bowl, cutlery, napkins
- aprons
- salt/pepper shakers
- coffee urn /teapot
- creamers/sugar packets
- butter dish

Preprogram Preparation

- Set your table with enough settings for the correct number of participants. Remember to plan for participants with long legs in wheel chairs to not sit opposite one another (footsies will ensue!)
- Prepare chicken dinner as per recipe (chicken needs to be in oven for a minimum 2.5 hours).
- Make at least one pot of coffee and/or tea prior to participants' arrival.

Procedure

1. Seat participants as previously planned. Begin dinner with coffee/ tea service (remember to check fluid restrictions to determine if thickened fluids are necessary).

2. Introduce your meal: When filling plate service, ensure that participants get *what* they want and *how much* they want (as dictated by dietary restrictions). Assist participants with meal activities—cutting, mashing, pouring—as required. The vegetables should be soft enough to mash to accommodate a soft/minced diet.

Physical

Decreased fine/gross motor skills, decreased vision: Assist participants to the degree they are comfortable. Have a volunteer/staff assist any participant who is visually impaired, either through assisted feeding, or by using the 'clock' method. (e.g., potatoes are at 1:00, chicken is at 6:00).

Cognitive

Can be used with any cognitive functioning level. If using with Alzheimer's participants, start with smaller portions and encourage second helpings. This program is a good opportunity to reminisce about individual cooking techniques, traditional family Sunday dinners, etc.

Social

If a participant exhibits low social mannerisms/problematic behaviors, use the opportunity to sit 1:1 with the participant and quietly partner with him or her to promote acceptable social behaviors.

Safety Issues

Dietary Restrictions

It is very important to know each participant's allergy alert(s) and fluid-level prior to participation. This program is not suitable for diets that require purée meals.

Aprons

Provide aprons to protect clothes from cooking supplies (cloth are most appropriate).

Tips and Tricks

- This meal works very well, as it requires minimal preparation time. It has been a huge hit every single time I have used it in a lunch group.
- Make sure your participants have their dentures in before arriving at the program!

Sunday Chicken Dinner

1	Frying Chicken
5 lb.	Potatoes
1	Large Onion
1	Lemon
2 lb.	Carrots
	salt, pepper, garlic powder (to taste)

Directions

1. Place chicken in roaster breast side up (a disposable foil roaster is handy—less dishes to wash!). If using foil roaster, cover chicken with tinfoil.
2. Cube potatoes (leave skins on—very tasty), approximately 2 to 3 inch sizes.
3. Slice carrots, approximately one quarter to one half inch thick.
4. Chop onion into bite-sized pieces (or leave big enough for participants to pick out).
5. Place potatoes, carrots and onion around all sides of chicken.
6. Make small slits in the skin of the chicken on the breast and legs. Place a wedge of lemon in each slit.
7. Pour 3 (4 if you plan on having gravy) cups of water over all the vegetables in the roaster.
8. Place lid on roaster (or tinfoil) and put in oven at 325° for 2.5 hours.

Option: Save half the potatoes for mashing. If adding the mashed option, cut potatoes in quarters and start to boil them for 45–60 minutes prior to program start.

GREETING GROUP GOODIES

Objective

To provide the opportunity to spread goodwill and cheer through the use of familiar baking skills

Targeted Domains and Benefits

Physical	hand–eye coordination, manual dexterity, muscle tone
Social	general conversation, sharing, peer support
Cognitive	sensory stimulation, sequential processing
Emotional	creating a feeling of goodwill, decreasing fear/ nervousness of new members

Preparation and Materials

- notify greeting group of upcoming need
- a small dessert bowl per person
- a butter knife per person
- a spoon per person
- ingredients

Procedure

1. Remind group of purpose: to bake a dozen "greetings" that can be taken by each group member to the new community member.
2. Using a premixed muffin mix (decreased prep time) bake a dozen muffins.
3. While waiting for muffins to finish baking (usually about 20 minutes), have each group member plan out how they will decorate their muffin with a welcome message.
4. Once muffins are cooled, slice in half and spread cream cheese on both sides of the muffin cut. Add one teaspoon of pie filling if desired. Place the two muffin pieces back together again.
5. Decorate the top of the muffin with leftover cream cheese icing and candies.

6. After muffins are decorated, have each participant take their muffin (not necessarily at the same time) to the new community member, or present the "greeting gift" as a group.

Modifications

Physical

Decreased fine/gross motor skills, decreased vision: Assist participants to the degree they are comfortable. The facilitator may have to do the actual mixing etc, but the participants can make decisions like reading the recipe, making sure the facilitator is following it correctly, and how much to pour into each muffin cup.

Cognitive

This program is best used with a high-functioning participant group, which allows the facilitator to be assured that each participant is capable of presenting their gift to the new community member without issue.

Social

If a group member does not want to be part of the greeting process, provide them the opportunity to decline that day's participation. Follow up with any participant who declines to determine if there is a problem behind their refusal, or if they are simply not interested in being part of the greeting time until further notice.

Safety Issues

Dietary Restrictions

The facilitator should confirm the new community member's diet to ensure that the muffins are an appropriate gift.

New Community Member Overwhelmed or Angry

Reassure your greeting group that their intentions were honorable and that perhaps by delaying the welcome by a day, or by dropping their gifts at different times, they may receive a more positive reaction.

Tips and Tricks

- This is a great way for higher functioning participants to get to know their new neighbor.
- This activity can ease the transition of a move for the new community member and foster positive social interactions in a short time frame.

- Suggested candies include chocolate covered raisins, plain raisins, Smarties, gummy bears.
- Print off small flags with greetings on them, tape to toothpicks, and stick in the muffin.

Cream Cheese Icing

1 250 g pkg	cream cheese
1/8 cup	butter
1 cup	powdered sugar

Directions

1. Mix cream cheese and butter together. Beat until smooth.
2. Add icing sugar, beating until smooth.

Optional: Replace cream cheese icing with whipped cream (canned, frozen, or fresh).

COW PATTIES

Objective

To stimulate long-term and short-term memory by using familiar skills

Targeted Domains and Benefits

Physical	hand–eye coordination, manual dexterity
Social	general conversation, sharing, peer support
Cognitive	sensory stimulation, measuring, following directions

Preparation and Materials

- purchase a bag of snacks (soft cheese twists are a hit)
- a tablespoon per person
- an apron per person
- ingredients
- wet/dry cloths (for clean up)

Procedure

1. Outline what the group procedure will be.
2. Hand out copies of the recipe.
3. Read through the recipe with the participants.
4. Ask for volunteers or assign, as necessary, a participant to each step in the recipe. Participants may choose just to measure, or only to stir, or only to watch.
5. Once roles have been assigned, work through the recipe with participants.
6. While the cookies are cooling in the freezer, compliment participants on how well they worked as a team and discuss how they feel about their teamwork. This is also an opportunity to have participants share their favorite recipe and do a little reminiscing. Pour coffee/juice for everyone and have some snacks on hand, as the cookies will need to cool prior to eating.

7. Near the end of the program, test the cookies. If the cookies are cooled and not runny, distribute one cookie to each resident. The remainder can be stored in a freezer for future use (within two weeks or until they lose their appeal).

Modifications

Physical

Decreased fine/gross motor skills, decreased vision: Assist participants to the degree they are comfortable. The facilitator may have to do the actual mixing etc, but the participants can make decisions like reading the recipe, making sure the facilitator is following it correctly, and how much to drop onto the cookie sheet.

Cognitive

If using this program with low-functioning group, ensure that stirring at the hot stove is done by a staff or volunteer, or assign 1:1 interaction and have a staff/volunteer assist the low-functioning participant in their stirring experience.

Social

Ensure that the action assigned to the participant is within their functional ability.

Safety Issues

Dietary Restrictions

Know your participants' allergies!

Stirring at Hot Stove

Know where your fire extinguisher is! Ensure that the participants are not wearing baggy clothing. They must also wear a fire-retardant apron. Have participants wear a flexible silicone (heat proof) oven mitt while stirring.

Tips and Tricks

- Tape foam around the handle of stirring spoons to make grasping easier—just make sure the foam is clean and pieces don't fall into the mix!

- A great "assembly line" recipe when working with high-functioning participants. Use this when making bulk-cookies for special events. This is always a popular sell at a bake sale too.

Cow Patties

1 cup	chocolate chips
5 tbps	butter or margarine
16	large marshmallows
1 tsp	vanilla extract
2 cups	rolled oats (quick or old fashioned, uncooked)
1 cup	raisins and/or nuts

Directions

1. Line baking sheets with wax paper.
2. Melt chocolate chips, butter, and large marshmallows in large saucepan over low heat; stir until smooth.
3. Remove from heat; cool slightly.
4. Stir in vanilla extract.
5. Stir in oats and remaining ingredients.
6. Drop by rounded teaspoonfuls onto prepared sheets.
7. Cover and refrigerate for two to four hours. Warm at room temperature for about 15 minutes before serving. Store tightly covered in refrigerator.

DREAMBOAT DESSERT

Objective

To stimulate long-term and short-term memory by using familiar skills

Targeted Domains and Benefits

Physical	hand–eye coordination, manual dexterity, increased muscle tone
Social	general conversation, sharing, peer support
Cognitive	sensory stimulation, sequential processing

Preparation and Materials

- an apron per person
- ingredients
- wet/dry cloths (for clean up)

Procedure

1. Hand out copies of the recipe.
2. Read through the recipe with the participants.
3. Ask for volunteers or assign, as necessary, a participant to each step in the recipe. Participants may choose just to measure, or only to stir, or only to watch.
4. Once roles have been assigned, work through the recipe with participants. (Note: Make the Jell-O mixture first—this allows the participants to continue working while the Jell-O sets. Use a 9x13 long pan for more dessert!)
5. Once the dessert is completed, place it in the fridge to allow it to cool/set (approximately 1/2 hour). During this time, pour coffee for participants, discuss the success of the program, and use the opportunity to reminisce about past occasions using desserts (e.g., church socials, family gatherings).

Modifications

Physical
Decreased fine/gross motor skills, decreased vision: Assist participants to the degree they are comfortable. Have group members assist each other. For example, one can measure and the other can stir.

Social
Ensure that the action assigned to the participant is within their functional ability.

Safety Issues

Dietary Restrictions
Know your participants' allergies!

Electric Mixer
Ensure participants are not wearing baggy sleeves (these can get caught in the mixer). If working with a low-functioning group, be vigilant in keeping fingers away from the beaters!

Tips and Tricks

- You will definitely want to use an electric mixer with this recipe. Usually I am the taskmaster and make everyone do all mixing by hand, but hand-mixing cream cheese is pushing it!
- This dessert is a big hit at special events (one pan can easily serve 20), and it can be low fat too!

Dreamboat Dessert

1 pkg (500 g)	cream cheese
1 pkg	flavored Jell-O (lime and raspberry work very well)
1 box	graham cracker crumbs
1 container	Dream Whip

Directions

1. Make Jell-O according to the directions on package. Place in fridge to partially set (will usually be perfect by time the rest of the recipe is ready).
2. Using graham cracker crumbs, make a base layer in the 9x13 pan approximately 1/4" deep.
3. Mix in one package of room temperature cream cheese with the container of whipped cream.

4. Take Jell-O from fridge and pour into cream cheese/whipped cream mixture.

5. Once completely mixed, place mixture on graham wafer layer—fill to top of pan.

6. Sprinkle graham wafer crumbs over top of mixture before placing in fridge to cool for 1/2 hour. Serve directly from pan.

TRAIL MIX

Objective

To stimulate long-term and short-term memory by using familiar skills

Targeted Domains and Benefits

Physical   hand–eye coordination, manual dexterity

Social   general conversation, sharing, peer support

Cognitive   sensory stimulation, sequential processing

Preparation and Materials

- an apron per person
- ingredients
- wet/dry cloths (for clean up)

Procedure

1. Hand out copies of the recipe. Read through the recipe with the participants. Ask for volunteers or assign, as necessary, a participant to each step in the recipe. Participants may choose just to measure or only to watch.
2. Once roles have been assigned, work through the recipe with participants. Place all the measured ingredients into a large mixing bowl and gently mix together. Once mixed, place mixture into freezer bags or small plastic containers with lids.

Modifications

Physical
Decreased fine/gross motor skills, decreased vision: Assist participants to the degree they are comfortable. Have group members assist each other. For example, one can measure and the other can stir.

Safety Issues

Dietary Restrictions
Know your participants' allergies! Make a nut-free mixture, if necessary.

Double Dipping
Watch that participants don't eat from their hands and then put hands back into ingredient bags (or that they don't eat it all before you are finished!).

Choking Risk
This recipe is best used with participants who have no swallowing concerns. Still, the best risk-management practice ensures that all participants are observed while eating.

Tips and Tricks

- Small yogurt containers with lids work well for traveling. The trail mix tends to be less crushed when in hard containers versus a plastic baggie. Put the whole mixture into one large container and dole out portions to all participants on the outing at the designated snack/meal time.

Trail Mix

1 package (1 kg)	chocolate covered raisins
2 packages (450 g)	shelled peanuts (salted or unsalted)
1 box	soft granola bars (any flavor)
1 package (1 kg)	chocolate chips
1 box (500 g)	wheat-based cereal
1 package (450 g)	pretzels (salted or unsalted)
1 package (250 g)	shelled sunflower seeds (salted or unsalted)

Directions

1. Measure out one cup of each of the first 4 ingredients. Place each measured cup into a large mixing bowl and mix lightly.
2. Add two cups of the wheat-based cereal to the mixing bowl.
3. Add three cups of pretzels to the mixing bowl and mix lightly.
4. After mixing the total ingredients thoroughly, place one cup of the mixture into a freezer bag or small plastic container.
5. Before sealing each mixture (you will have 10 bags), place a handful of sunflower seeds on top of each.
6. If putting the whole mixture into one container, keep the sunflower seeds separate and add just before eating.

LEAVE YOUR TEETH BEHIND

Objective

To stimulate long- and short-term memory by using familiar skills

Targeted Domains and Benefits

Physical	hand–eye coordination, manual dexterity
Social	general conversation, sharing, peer support
Cognitive	sensory stimulation, sequential processing

Preparation and Materials

- an apron per person
- ingredients

Procedure

1. Hand out copies of the recipe.
2. Read through the recipe with the participants. Ask for volunteers or assign, as necessary, a participant to each step in the recipe. Participants may choose just to measure or only to watch.
3. Once roles have been assigned, work through the recipe with participants.
4. Have a prebaked cake available (bake before hand) to decrease waiting time.
5. Create teams and place them in charge of each layer: one team for fruit, one team for cake crumble, one team for whipped cream.
6. Once recipe is completed, set out bowls for everyone and get right to eating!

Modifications

Physical
Decreased fine/gross motor skills, decreased vision: Assist participants to the degree they are comfortable. Have group members assist each other. For example, one can measure and the other can stir.

Swallowing Difficulties

Do not use fruit. Once the trifle is in an individual's dish, mash thoroughly with a fork and add extra whipped cream mixture to thicken and moisten if necessary.

Safety Issues

Dietary Restrictions

Know each participant's diet—this dessert can be mashed into a thickened purée consistency if necessary. Be aware of any food allergies.

Tips and Tricks

- Use a glass trifle bowl—the colors are pretty when viewing it from the outside.
- Use pie filling (sparingly!) instead of real fruit. Mash the pie filling/fruit before spooning it into the trifle. Mashed fresh fruit can also be used, such as melons, small berries, and plums.

Leave Your Teeth Behind

1 package (500 g)	cream cheese (room temperature)
1 container (500 g)	Cool Whip
2 cans	crushed pineapple and juice
1	premade cake (angel food is a nice one to use)

Directions

1. Drain the juice from the pineapple, saving the juice from one can. Set pineapple aside.
2. Using an electric mixer, mix the cream cheese, whipped cream and pineapple juice together. Use discretion when adding juice—add just enough to make sure the mixture is not watery (if it is too watery, add more cream cheese).
3. Crumble the cake into bite sized pieces.
4. Using the trifle dish, begin with a thick layer of cake at the bottom of the dish and press pieces together firmly on bottom layer.
5. Add the cream cheese mixture on top of the cake.
6. Add a light layer of crushed pineapple (or fruit of choice) on top of cream cheese.
7. Add another layer of cake, but do not press flat.
8. Repeat steps 5 through 7 until the dish is full or until ingredients are used up.
9. Chill in refrigerator for 15 minutes before serving.

VEGETARIAN PEPPER MASH

Objective

To use tactile stimulation (smell/taste) to improve food intake

Targeted Domains and Benefits

Physical	hand–eye coordination, manual dexterity, fine motor skills
Social	general conversation, reinforcing positive table manners
Cognitive	reminiscing, sensory stimulation
Emotional	creating a family-style gathering, fostering emotional growth of group

Preparation and Materials

- decorate eating area as a "home-styled" kitchen (tablecloths, pretty napkins, matching dinnerware—not plastic!)
- a place setting (plate, cutlery, napkin) per person
- an apron per person
- salt/pepper
- coffeepot/teapot
- cream and sugar
- butter

Procedure Prior to Session

1. Set your table with enough settings for the correct number of participants.
2. Prepare baked peppers as per recipe (1/2 hour prep time, 1/2 hour cook time).
3. Make at least one pot of coffee and one pot of tea prior to participants' arrival.

Procedure

1. Begin dinner with coffee/tea service (remember to check fluid restrictions to determine if thickened fluids are necessary).

2. Introduce your meal: When filling plate service, ensure that participants get *what* they want and *how much* they want (as dictated by dietary restrictions).

3. Assist participants with meal activities—cutting, mashing, pouring—as required. The vegetables should be soft enough to mash to accommodate a soft/minced diet.

Modifications

Physical

Decreased fine/gross motor skills, decreased vision: Assist participants to the degree they are comfortable. Have a volunteer/staff assist any participant who is visually impaired, either through assisted feeding or by using the 'clock' method (e.g., fork is at 3:00).

Cognitive

This program can be used with any cognitive functioning level, as it provides a good opportunity to reminisce about cooking techniques, other vegetarian dishes, etc.

Social

If a participant exhibits low social mannerisms/problematic behaviors, use the opportunity to sit 1:1 with the participant and quietly partner with him or her to promote acceptable social behaviors.

Safety Issues

Dietary Restrictions

It is very important to know participants' allergy alerts and fluid-level prior to participation. This activity is not suitable for diets that require purée meals. Ensure that peppers are cooled enough so participants will not burn their mouths.

Aprons

Provide aprons to protect clothes while eating (cloth are most appropriate, or linen napkins).

Tips and Tricks

- Participants get a kick out of being able to eat their whole dinner—container and all.

Vegetarian Pepper Mash

1 box instant rice
1 package frozen vegetables
1 green or red pepper per participant
1 large can tomato soup
1 large onion (finely chopped)
seasonings to taste

Directions

1. Cut tops off peppers (saving tops) and scrape seeds out of each pepper.
2. Prepare six cups of instant rice according to directions on box.
3. Chop onion into fine pieces.
4. When rice is finished, add vegetables and finely chopped onion, and season mixture to taste.
5. Set rice mixture aside and prepare large can of tomato soup according to directions on label.
6. Set soup aside and allow to cool.
7. While soup is cooling, stuff each pepper 3/4 full with the rice mixture.
8. Pour 1/2 cup of tomato soup on top of rice mixture and replace pepper tops.
9. Bake peppers in oven for 15–20 minutes at 275° F.
10. Remove from oven and serve immediately.

VEGETARIAN CROISSANT DELIGHT

Objective

To stimulate long-term and short-term memory by using familiar skills

Targeted Domains and Benefits

Physical	hand–eye coordination, manual dexterity
Social	general conversation, sharing, peer support
Cognitive	sensory stimulation, sequential processing, identifying different materials

Preparation and Materials

- an apron per person
- frozen croissant dough
- spinach
- block cheese

Procedure

1. Hand out copies of the recipe.
2. Read through the recipe with the participants. Ask for volunteers or assign, as necessary, a participant to each step in the recipe. Participants may choose just to measure or only to watch.
3. Wash the spinach and gently pat dry with a paper towel. Slice cheese into thin strips (any cheese works well—Brie is a real treat!) Once roles have been assigned, work through the recipe with participants. Eat these fresh out of the oven. This is a lovely side dish for the vegetarian pepper mash!

Modifications

Physical

Decreased fine/gross motor skills, decreased vision: Have these participants man the "spinach patrol"—they can wash, dry and tear the spinach.
Dietary restrictions: Be aware of each participant's allergies and swallowing assessment.

Safety Issues

Dietary Restrictions

This recipe is not suitable for a gluten-free diet.

Tips and Tricks

- Use a cheese cutter board, as this allows all levels of functioning participants the opportunity to be involved in cutting the cheese. If using Brie, simply cut by hand.
- Change the vegetarian options. Try using mushrooms, onion, salsa, or peppers.
- Have a lunch group work on creating these rolls while a staff member prepares the vegetarian pepper mash.
- This recipe can be made nonvegetarian by adding any type of sliced meat into the croissant. If using more filling, use two triangles per croissant: one for the base, then the fillings, and then one triangle on top. Do not roll the mixture; simply bake as per instructions on croissant package. This then becomes more of a meal than a side dish.

Vegetarian Croissant Delight

1 pkg	prepared croissant dough
1 head	fresh spinach
500 g	yellow cheese

Directions

1. Roll out the prepared croissant dough into triangles.
2. Place two leaves of fresh spinach (ripped to size) and two thin slices of yellow cheese in the center of each triangle.
3. Roll up the dough, keeping the spinach and cheese on the inside.
4. Place the dough on baking tray.
5. When all triangles have been rolled, place tray in oven and bake as per instructions on the croissant package. Remove from oven and serve fresh.

SECTION 4

CRAFTY CREATIONS

Crafts can be a goldmine…or a nightmare. With these plans, your nightmares will end and your creative juices will start flowing.

Take a look in your storage area—there are probably boxes of donated supplies you never quite figured out what to do with. Do not despair—these items can and will be used. There is never a "white elephant" in a recreation department!

Many of these plans use simple materials, many of which can be donated. For this reason, it is important to make a wish-list. Families always ask what they can do and this is your opportunity to build up your craft supplies. Keep a running inventory of what you use the most and how frequently it needs to be stocked. This will allow you to add to your wish list in plenty of time for donations to come in.

Most of all, enjoy the creativity of the participants. There is nothing like seeing beaming faces after they have created a personal work of art for themselves or, more often than not, as a gift for someone they care about.

ELF BLOCKS

Objective

To make a decorative craft for display or for use as a tree ornament

Targeted Domains and Benefits

Physical	hand–eye coordination, manual dexterity, fine motor skills, muscle tone
Social	sharing equipment, general conversation, peer support
Cognitive	sequential processing, decision making, identifying colors and shapes
Emotional	creative expression, increased self-esteem and feelings of accomplishment

Preparation and Materials

- pre-cut the required materials for each elf block and sort into individual packages
- make samples (for viewing and personal knowledge!)
- set up chairs and tables, placing the pre-made packages at each chair
- set up a cutting board (or a metal pan) in the center of each table for glue guns, accompanied by 20 glue sticks for each gun provided
- a set of felt cut-outs per person: hat, collar, arms, legs, wooden bead head, mall bell, (4) medium pom-poms in coordinating colors, wooden letter block
- an apron per person
- glue guns
- glue sticks
- small dowels
- popsicle sticks

Procedure During Session

Note: Pattern pieces can be found in the Appendix, page 178.

Modifications

Physical

Parkinson's, Stroke, Visual Impairment: Provide larger supplies (double the original pattern/block size). Hint: Red or pink increases the degree of vision for certain types of visual impairment. For stroke, place all materials on the strong side and place the participant near the facilitator or assign a volunteer or coresident "buddy" to assist. To manage a participant with tremors, place them near the facilitator to monitor the degree of tremors and to assist as necessary. Have the facilitator or an assigned "buddy" place hot glue on popsicle stick. Provide extra time for completion based on the tremors' effect on participation.

Cognitive

Dementia: Do not prepackage materials. Take materials for participants to sort into groupings. The sorting itself becomes a program within a program. Once all materials are sorted, assist participants in identifying the next step. The facilitator then glues the items as required. For low functioning residents, the facilitator can help them make choices but may have to physically put the craft together while involving the client through conversation and guided imagery.

Safety Issues

Glue Gun

This is a hazardous piece of equipment even at the best of times. If necessary, have a volunteer/aide place the dollops of glue needed for each step on the small popsicle stick/dowel rod of each participant. Make sure the glue gun is placed on a nonscorching surface, such as metal cookie sheets or ceramic tile. Use low-temperature bonding glue for less chance of serious burns. A cordless glue-gun is very helpful.

Extension Cords

Make sure extension cords are either completely out of the walking path or range of motion of every participant, or taped down if this option is not available.

Aprons

While this is not necessarily safety oriented, aprons can be worn to protect clothes from flyaway glue strands.

Tips and Tricks

- Put out a request through a wish list (made available to staff, families, and the general public) at least three months before the materials area needed. Many people have these types of supplies lying around and are even willing to buy inexpensive items to donate.

- Contact a local craft store to see if they would be willing to sponsor this craft—an excellent prospect to consider during the Christmas season.

- Assign volunteers to contact "x" amount of people, who then contact "x" amount of people in a supply blitz. Each person in the chain expands the network that much further. You'll be amazed at what people will drop off! I asked for yarn and ribbon and ended up with an organ.

- Contact your local contracting store (e.g., Home Depot) or commercial printing shop to see if they will donate work aprons to your program. This will minimize costs considerably.

GARDEN BUDDIES

Objective

To provide an opportunity to express oneself using personal creativity

Targeted Domains and Benefits

Physical	hand–eye coordination, gross/fine motor control
Social	sharing equipment, general conversation, peer support
Cognitive	sequential processing, identifying colors
Emotional	creative expression, emotional expression of artwork

Preparation and Materials

- an apron per person
- a pair latex gloves per person
- a paintbrush per person
- plain newsprint paper
- rock(s) (fist-sized or larger work well)
- pill cups or small yogurt containers
- variety of craft materials: glitter glue, felt, fabric swatches, wiggly eyes, yarn, felt, pipe cleaners
- hot glue guns (cordless is great)
- glue sticks
- scissors

Procedure

1. Clean the rocks prior to program.
2. Place acrylic paints and paintbrushes within easy reach of the participants.
3. Provide participants with an apron, gloves, and a water cup for rinsing their brush.
4. Place accessories (pipe cleaners, yarn, wiggly eyes, fabric, glitter glue, felt) in the center of the table.

5. Have participants select a rock they would like to use and place it in front of them. Tape newsprint (or any other scrap paper) underneath the rocks to minimize cleanup.

6. Have participants select different materials/accessories they would like to put on their rock. Use gentle cueing/prompting if no immediate selections made.

7. Paint details first, then use accessories to complete the project (i.e., paint on nose and ears, then add red felt for lips, wiggly eyes, yarn for hair). It is at the participants discretion if they want to use only paint or a combination of all available materials.

8. If using materials other than paint, the facilitator can use the hot glue gun to attach materials to the rock.

9. Once completed, hot glue small strips of felt to the bottom of the rock in order to prevent scratching/slipping on sitting surface. The rocks can be used as accents in indoor or outdoor gardens. If using in an outdoor setting, be sure to use acrylic spray to seal the rocks before placing them outside.

Modifications

Physical
Parkinson's, Stroke, Visual Impairment: If using standard brushes, tape foam around the handles for a larger grip area. For stroke, place all materials on the strong side and place the client near the facilitator, or assign a volunteer or coresident "buddy" to assist. To manage a participant with tremors, place the participant near the facilitator to monitor degree of tremors and assist as necessary. To manage visual impairment, seat that participant nearest the facilitator, or assign a volunteer as able, to work 1:1 with that participant.

Cognitive
Dementia: Watch for participants who may try to ingest materials. In this situation, use some backup rocks and assign a volunteer/staff member to work 1:1 with that participant to re-wash the rocks.

Safety Issues

Glue Gun
Only staff members should use the glue-gun and a low-temperature bonding glue (for less chance of serious burns). A cordless glue-gun is very helpful.

Aprons
These are vital to protect clothes against paint splatters—acrylic DOES NOT always wash out!

Tips and Tricks

- Use old, somewhat faded/stained fabric tablecloths lying around (contact a Ladies Auxiliary at a local church and see if they have any old ones they would be willing to donate). Cut them into large rectangles, fold in half, and cut a large neck hole. This is not necessarily the fanciest, but they work well!

- The rocks can be any size, but those with a flat enough bottom that they won't roll around while painting work best—check out construction sites for free rocks.

- Ask for donated yarn—it makes great hair to glue-gun to top of the rocks.

POT HEADS

Objective

To provide an opportunity for self-expression using personal creativity

Targeted Domains and Benefits

Physical	hand–eye coordination, gross/fine motor control
Social	sharing equipment, general conversation, peer support
Cognitive	sequential processing, decision making, identifying colors
Emotional	creative expression, emotional expression of artwork

Preparation and Materials

- an apron per person
- a pair latex gloves per person
- a paintbrush per person
- plain newsprint paper
- terra-cotta plant pot
- pill cups or small yogurt containers
- a selection of paint
- variety of craft materials: glitter glue, felt, fabric swatches, wiggly eyes, yarn, felt, pipe cleaners
- grass seed
- soil
- hot glue guns (cordless is great)
- glue sticks
- scissors

Procedure Prior to Session

1. Before taking the materials to the program, hot-glue wiggly eyes onto each pot.

2. Set up a table covered in newsprint.

3. Provide each participant with a pot, paintbrush, and a selection of paint.

4. Participants may use rubber stamps or freehand paint the other side of the pot as well.

Procedure

1. Seat participants around a table with the materials ready at each place setting.

2. Have each participant embellish the pot using available materials, working around the wiggly eyes to create a face.

3. Have extra pots available as back-ups in case they finish quickly and require another project pot.

4. Put soil in a plastic bag or ice-cream bucket in the center of the table.

5. Assist participants in filling their chosen pot with dirt to approximately 1" from top of pot.

6. Sprinkle a liberal amount of grass seed on top of the dirt.

7. Lightly cover the seed with a thin layer of soil and lightly tamp down with fingers.

8. Water the pots immediately.

9. Place the pots in the sunshine and water as needed over the following days/weeks.

10. Within a short time-frame, the grass will sprout, creating "hair" for each painted pot face.

Modifications

Physical

Stroke, Visual Impairment, Spasticity: If using standard brushes, tape foam around the handles for a larger grip area. For stroke, place all materials on the strong side and place the participant near the facilitator, or assign a volunteer or coresident "buddy" to assist. To manage participants with spasticity, have them make individual choices as to painting options (brush versus rubber stamps) and hold the pot while they paint to alleviate risk of breakage. Pre-fill the pot with dirt and have participants add the grass seed. To manage visual impairment, seat that participant nearest the facilitator (or assign a volunteer as able) to work 1:1 with him or her.

Cognitive

Dementia: Watch for participants who may try to ingest materials. For participants at risk for this type of behavior, assign a staff member or volunteer to work alongside these participants for the duration of the program.

Safety Issues

Pot Breakage

Have broom/dustpan available in the event of broken pots.

Tips and Tricks

- This activity works best in a non-carpeted area. If this is not an option, lay sheets of newsprint around the work area prior to the start of the program. Remember to clean up any spilled materials—you won't make any friends in housekeeping if you leave your mess behind!

- These potheads make very cheerful additions to an indoor winter garden area. Our potheads have created many a smile!

TIN LID ORNAMENTS

Objective

To provide an opportunity for self-expression using personal creativity

Targeted Domains and Benefits

Physical	hand–eye coordination, gross/fine motor control, muscle tone
Social	sharing equipment, general conversation, peer support
Cognitive	sequential processing, decision making
Emotional	creative expression, emotional expression of artwork

Preparation and Materials

- an apron per person
- a pair latex gloves per person
- a pair safety goggles per person
- tin lids from frozen juices
- nails
- old wood
- hot glue guns (cordless is great)
- glue sticks
- scissors
- raffia
- fabric pieces
- a ball peen hammer

Procedure Prior to Session

1. Wash lids thoroughly with soap and water. Rinse well and dry.
2. Make a sample for all participants to see prior to starting program.
3. Create simple line art templates of words such as JOY, LOVE, and HI for participants to follow (see Appendix, page 179).

Procedure

1. Show participants a sample and briefly explain the process of creating the project.
2. Have participants select their choice of raffia and fabric.
3. Measure the circumference of the lid and cut the raffia to match, leaving 1/2" to overlap (approximately 9.25" to 9.5" long).
4. Twist the raffia loosely and have participants hold it at the top (12:00) while the facilitator hot-glues the bottom (6:00). Hot glue the top pieces, making sure to overlap slightly.
5. Lightly glue the sides (3:00 and 9:00) to hold them in place.
6. Take a 4" strip of raffia (the same or a different color) and make a figure eight, with the two ends jutting out past the figure eight (it should look like a bow).
7. Using a thin piece of fabric, tightly tie a knot around the figure eight bow and leave a bit of fabric dangling below the bow.
8. Lightly hot glue the ribbon to the top part of the lid, making sure to cover the overlapping pieces from the outside edge raffia piece.
9. Tape the premade word templates to the front of the lid and place the ornament on top of the old piece of wood (no nail holes in the table this time!).
10. Using a hammer and nail, lightly pound the nail (just hard enough to go through the lid) following the inside of the letter outline (or use a freehand style).
11. Once the letters are punched, remove the template and the ornament is complete!

Modifications

Physical
Visual Impairment, CNS Disorders: Have participants with visual impairment make the selections they desire. A staff member/volunteer can do the hands on work. Remember to visually describe what is happening at all stages of the program. Physical stability may vary for participants with any central nervous system disorder. Encourage participants to make choices and to physically do what they are comfortable doing, however; a staff member/volunteer will more than likely have to do the nail-punching (as a risk management practice).

Cognitive
This program is most suitable for mid to high-range functioning participants.

Safety Issues

Burns
Only staff members/volunteers should be assigned to glue gun duty.

Nail Punching
Make sure that participants do not hit their own fingers/hands with the hammer.

Tips and Tricks

- Use long-nosed rubber-grip tweezers (these can be found in medical supply stores or ask your local physician) to hold the nail while nail punching. This decreases the risk of smashed fingers and broken fingernails!

- You may want to prepunch the lids if working with a low-functioning group. This decreases the safety hazard, and saves time.

- Ask everyone you know to save juice lids and leftover fabric for you. Check with fabric stores for donated remnants to your program.

Fuzzy Tactile Dice

Objective

To provide an opportunity for personal expression through the creation of three-dimensional objects

Targeted Domains and Benefits

Physical	hand–eye coordination, gross/fine motor control
Social	interaction skills, sharing equipment, general conversation, peer support
Cognitive	sequential processing, decision making, identifying texture

Preparation and Materials

- an apron per person
- a pencil per person
- a measuring tape or ruler per person
- hot glue guns (cordless is great)
- glue sticks
- scissors
- fabric swatches
- black felt
- duct tape (silver-threaded is best)
- cardboard
- regular dice

Procedure

1. Lay a collection of flattened cardboard boxes in the center of the table (1/2" thick maximum). Ensure that there is enough cardboard to make five complete dice.

2. Divide the group into two teams.

3. Have each team select a piece of cardboard and measure out a rectangle 36" long by 12" wide. Cut the cardboard to size (using strong scissors).

4. Using the ruler, measure off 12" squares (3 squares per cut piece) and mark each 12" section with a pencil line.

5. Open up the scissors and, using one blade, lightly score (cut into) the pencil line to assist with folding.

6. Once both pencil lines are scored, bend the cardboard to create a 3-section strip.

7. Repeat steps 3 to 7 once more, finishing with two 3-section strips.

8. Fold the first piece into a "U" shape, and have one team member hold it steady.

9. Have the second team member take the second piece, fold it into a "U" shape, and place it upside down and sideways over the first piece to create a solid cube shape.

10. While both team members hold their pieces in place, the facilitator uses the duct tape to secure each side where the two pieces meet. Don't be shy with the tape—the cubes need to be taped very well in order to hold up for a long period of use.

11. Once the cube has been completed, each team measures out six different blocks of fabric (12.5" square, allowing for a quarter inch overlap) and glues the squares of fabric to each side of the cube.

12. Next, glue the quarter inch trim down on the first two sides— excess edges can be trimmed off on the last four sides. Don't be afraid to use the glue—the fabric needs to stay on for a very long time!

13. After the fabric has been glued to all six sides of the cube, each team cuts out 21 three-inch circles out of black felt.

14. Glue each of the circles to the appropriate sides to recreate a single die (use the small playing dice as a visual sample).

Modifications

Physical

Visual Impairment, Stroke, MS, Parkinson's: Assign the fabric swatch choices to those participants unable to physically assist in the creation process. Involve them in the creation process by asking questions and have them monitor for size and straightness.

Cognitive

This project is most suitable for mid to high-range functioning participants. If using with low-functioning participants or Dementia participants, precut the cardboard, make one die at a time, and limit your group size to three. Involve the dementia participants through choices, playing with fabric samples, cutting circles (as appropriate).

Safety Issues

Burns
Only staff members/volunteers should be assigned to glue gun duty.

Scissors
Monitor participants as they use scissors to reduce the risk of injury.

Tips and Tricks

- The object is for the dice to be tactile—use fabrics like fake fur, those with textures (chenille), and stretchy rubber-like fabric. This can be a bit expensive, so put these items on a donation wish-list and ask at local fabric stores for donations. Remember to use fabric that will ensure the black dots can be seen easily.

- If purchasing fabric is out of your budget, use wallpaper with different designs. Ask a wallpaper store if you can have last year's wallpaper sample books. Hot glue the wallpaper, as the pre-glued wallpaper doesn't stick to cardboard for very long, if at all.

TWIG FRAMES

Objective

To provide an opportunity for personal expression through the creation of three-dimensional objects

Targeted Domains and Benefits

Physical	hand–eye coordination, gross/fine motor control
Social	sharing equipment, general conversation, peer support
Cognitive	sequential processing, decision making, identifying objects/textures
Emotional	interacting with nature, feelings of accomplishment, thinking of others

Preparation and Materials

- an apron per person
- an ice cream pail per person
- a plain wooden picture frame per person
- a pair of safety goggles per person
- collection of sticks
- hot glue guns (cordless is great)
- glue sticks
- a butter knife
- collections of old calendars
- a digital camera

Procedure

1. Take the group outside and go for a walk in a treed area to collect twigs and/or nature-like items from the ground (never break living twigs off a tree or shrub).
2. Have each participant collect objects that appeal to them and place their collected items in their pail or bag.
3. Take pictures of the group as they are in the process of collecting, or take individual shots in the treed area before returning indoors.

4. Once the group has collected a tidy amount of nature's gifts, return to program area to start making picture frames.

5. In the program area, seat participants at a table with plenty of elbow room.

6. Give each participant a small wooden frame.

7. Measure the length of the sticks (they should be uneven, more natural that way) to overlap the frame width, making sure not to block out too much of the picture area.

8. Wearing safety goggles, use the butter knife and hold the twig at the breaking-off point while pulling up on the other end of the twig to break it to size (or use strong scissors to cut to size).

9. Once the sticks are broken, glue twigs on the wooden border of the frame. Start in the middle of the top (long) side and place the sticks so that the greater length of the stick is on the outside of the frame. Continue working around the frame until it is completely covered.

10. If the participants have collected berries, glued them on top of the twigs afterward.

11. Pinecones can be glued across the twigs on the corners to hide the corner gaps.

12. Allow the frame to dry over night before inserting picture.

13. After the frames are completed, take photos of the participants if you have not already done so, or have participants select a picture from a collection of old calendars they would like to cut to size to fit in the frame.

Modifications

Physical
Visual Impairment, Stroke, MS, Parkinson's: For those in wheelchairs, assign a "buddy" from the group to collect items for the wheelchair participant who is unable to walk through the grass and over roots. Staff members/volunteers may have to assist with twig breaking and gluing for those exhibiting tremors or rigidity.

Cognitive
Dementia: Collect sufficient materials prior to the program and then either a) choose not to take participants outside, or b) scatter pre-collected twigs in a secure outside area and then take participants into the secure area to "collect" twigs.

Safety Issues

Elopement
Know your participants and their individual elopement risk indicator.

Scissors
Monitor the participants as they use scissors to reduce risk of injury.

Tips and Tricks

- My population is surrounded by a wide, dangerous open area, so I usually pick option "b" when doing nature-type activities because it gives me the opportunity to interact with a larger group that can include those with a high elopement indicator.

- Make rubbings of leaves with color pencils/regular pencils and use that as the piece of artwork for the frame.

- The most inexpensive wooden frames I have found have been at IKEA. Reduce costs by making heavy cardboard frames and taping lighter cardboard as a backing board to keep the picture in. Finally, glue string onto the back for hanger.

Holiday Picture Frames (2-part program)

Objective

To provide an opportunity for personal expression through the creation of three-dimensional objects

Targeted Domains and Benefits

Physical	hand–eye coordination, gross/fine motor control
Social	sharing equipment, general conversation, peer support
Cognitive	sequential processing, decision making
Emotional	feelings of accomplishment, thinking of others

Preparation and Materials

- an apron per person
- a pair latex gloves per person
- a paintbrush per person
- a water cup per person
- hot glue guns (cordless is great)
- glue sticks
- lightweight cardboard
- scissors
- clear tape
- a digital camera
- old newsprint
- acrylic paints
- puzzle pieces
- white glue (optional)
- ribbon

Procedure During First Session

1. Collect old puzzle pieces and place in large box in the center of the working area.
2. Tape down old newsprint over the working table.

3. Place large amounts of red and green acrylic paints in paint cups (saucers work well) and place them between every two participants.

4. Flip puzzle pieces to nonprinted (cardboard) side and paint a large amount of pieces green, with a few pieces painted red. After painting a selection of pieces, move them to the center of the working table to dry and continue until all pieces are painted.

5. Using lightweight cardboard, use the supplied template to cut out a cardboard ring 3.5" in diameter (save the centers—you will need them later!).

6. Cut an extra 3.5" solid cardboard circle (do not cut out the centers) for each frame.

7. Place all cardboard pieces into a bag to avoid misplacing any pieces.

8. Take pictures of each of your participants and print them on a color printer.

Procedure During Second Session

1. Ensure that each participant has two round frames.

2. Using the previously painted puzzle pieces, glue one layer around entire circumference of the cardboard frame.

3. If using hot glue, continue with a second layer, placing the second layer pieces over the places where each piece of the first layer meets. If using white glue, allow ten minutes for the first layer to dry before continuing with the second layer.

4. After completing the first frame, repeat steps 1 to 3 for second frame.

5. By the time the second frame is completed, the first will be dry enough to insert the participant's picture.

6. Using the center cutout as a template, trace a circle around the picture.

7. Cut one quarter inch outside of the pencil line and glue picture onto the solid 3.5" circle.

8. Placing glue around the outside edge of the picture circle, affix this piece to the back of the cardboard frame with the picture facing forwards.

9. Cut a piece of ribbon approximately seven inches long and hot glue it onto the back of the completed frame.

Modifications

Physical

Visual Impairment, Parkinson's, Stroke: Tape puzzle pieces onto newsprint (using clear tape) to stop pieces from moving while the participants are painting. Use verbal cueing to assist the visually impaired participants when placing puzzle pieces on cardboard.

Safety Issues

Scissors

Monitor the participants as they use scissors to reduce risk of injury.

Burns

Only staff members/volunteers should be assigned to glue gun duty.

Tips and Tricks

- Old puzzles are great donation requests—or you can pick them up at second hand stores and garage sales for next to nothing.
- These make nice year-to-year comparisons for participants and/or their families. My residents enjoy making these as gifts for family members at Christmas. The participant's picture can be replaced with a picture from old greeting cards, calendars and the like.
- Recycle the cardboard from office supply packing boxes and packages.

BEAUTIFUL GOODIE BAGS

Objective

To provide an opportunity for personal expression through the creation of a useful object

Targeted Domains and Benefits

Physical	hand–eye coordination, gross/fine motor control
Social	sharing equipment, general conversation, peer support
Cognitive	sequential processing, identifying colors, textures, patterns
Emotional	feelings of accomplishment, satisfaction in completion of project

Preparation and Materials

- an apron per person
- 4-inch wide wire craft ribbon
- color-coordinated thin ribbon
- individually wrapped chocolate pieces
- glue gun
- glue sticks

Procedure

1. Place a collection of 4-inch wire craft ribbon, thin ribbon, and chocolates in the center of the work area.
2. Have participants select which kind of 4-inch ribbon they would like to use.
3. Cut 5-inch strips of the selected wire ribbon and hot glue the long sides together. One end should remain open.
4. Have participants select the color of thin ribbon they would like to use.
5. Cut a 5-inch section of thin ribbon.
6. Place two individually wrapped chocolates inside the bag and, using the thin ribbon, tie a bow around the open end of the bag.

Modifications

Physical
Visual Impairment: Visually describe the pattern of the ribbon available to these participants and allow them to select their choice.

Cognitive
Dementia: Use only one pattern of ribbon and a coordinating thin ribbon.

Safety Issues

Scissors
Monitor the participants as they use scissors to reduce risk of injury.

Burns
Only staff members/volunteers should be assigned to glue gun duty.

Tips and Tricks

- Anything can be put into these bags. I've used them as Dream Builders in January, in which each participant writes out a dream or goal for the year and places it into the bag. At Christmas the participants can write out their Christmas wish, put it into the bag and then hang it on the tree (tie on a second, longer piece of ribbon to hang it with).
- If using chocolates, the bags make a nice table favors at Christmas parties.

WARPED VINYL ART

Objective

To provide an opportunity for personal expression through the creation of a useful object

Targeted Domains and Benefits

Physical	hand–eye coordination, gross/fine motor control
Social	sharing equipment, general conversation, peer support
Cognitive	sequential processing, decision making
Emotional	feelings of accomplishment and pleasure in creating art

Preparation and Materials

- an apron per person
- silicon oven mitts (for facilitator)
- a face mask (for spray painter)
- coffee can(s)
- selection of vinyl records
- spray paint
- glass beads/rocks
- stickers
- old cookie sheets

Note: If melting more than three records in one program, it is best to use a well-ventilated area. Open the windows, turn on an exhaust fan, and monitor the room for growing fumes.

Procedure

1. Place all shared materials in containers in the center of the working area.
2. Preheat oven to 200° F.
3. One participant at a time, center a vinyl record over the upside

down (open end down) coffee can. The label should be sitting in the center of the coffee can bottom. Balance the record so that it extends out evenly from all sides of the can.

4. Place the can and record on the old cookie sheet and gently slide them into the oven, being careful not to disturb the placement of the record on the can.

5. Bake for approximately 1–5 minutes, watching through the oven doors as the record starts to melt (it bends instead of dripping). Pull the record out of the oven when the participant determines it is the shape they desire. Do not melt it past the recommended heating time.

6. Have the participants back away from the oven and use the silicone gloves to pull out the cookie sheet with the melted record. Place them in a safe area away from the participants to cool—this takes approximately one minute. When it cools, the record will be as hard as it was originally.

7. Repeat steps 4 through 6 for each participant.

8. Once all participants have their cooled "art deco" in front of them, it is time to begin decorating the artwork. If participants choose to spray paint their artwork first, have a staff member/volunteer take it into an outside area and spray the artwork on old newsprint. Allow it to dry completely.

9. If not using spray paint, participants can use stickers, plastic/glass beads (the decorative "stones" for vases look very neat hot glued on), or any other available decorative item to individualize their creation.

Modifications

Physical
Visual Impairment: Visually describe the project and the process as it happens while that participant's art is in the oven. Assign a staff member/volunteer/participant buddy to assist with decorating choices.

Cognitive
Dementia: Make the actual artwork with a higher-functioning group and take the completed pieces into your dementia program to be decorated.

Safety Issues

Vinyl/Oven Burns
Only staff members/volunteers should put their hands in the oven.

Burns
Only staff members/volunteers should be assigned to glue gun duty.

Fumes
If melting 3 or more records, ensure that you are in a well-ventilated area with an inflow of fresh air. Monitor your space for increasing fumes. Stop immediately if the fumes become noticeable and introduce fresh air into the space.

Tips and Tricks

- Eyelash yarn looks good when glued around the top edges of the artwork.
- These can make nifty, stylish planter pots. Leave the hole open in the bottom center (the original hole in the middle) and use a regular bottom water tray to catch the drip through. Fill with dirt and funky flowers and voilá!, art deco lives again!
- If using spray paint, the staff members/volunteers can tie an old tea towel around their faces, or you can always pinch some paper masks from the nursing unit!
- A good place to find stickers of all sorts is in the "teacher's section" at office supply stores.
- Use your wish list to ask for the glass stones, spray paint, records, and stickers. Ten to one says you will end up with more records than you know what to do with!
- These pieces sell well at craft sales, especially when they are decorated with fun fur and other funky textiles.

Decorative Fabric Hangers

Objective

To provide an opportunity for personal expression through the creation of art

Targeted Domains and Benefits

Physical	hand–eye coordination, gross/fine motor control
Social	sharing equipment, general conversation, peer support
Cognitive	sequential processing, decision making, identifying and selecting materials
Emotional	feelings of accomplishment and pleasure in creating art

Preparation and Materials

- scissors
- straight pins
- sturdy stick from a tree
- sewing needles
- selection of material squares
- thread
- natural fiber twine
- a sewing machine
- small grommets (any color)
- an iron

Procedure

1. Place all shared materials in containers in the center of the working area.
2. Have participants take a walk outside to collect two sticks (the thickness of a finger) each.
3. Once participants are back at table, hand out scissors and straight pins to each of them.
4. Have participants select a variety of materials (colors, patterns, textures) and cut out 4.5 inch squares of fabric.

5. Take two pieces of fabric, and (right side in) use straight pins to pin them together.

6. Stitch three sides only, approximately 1/4" from the edge. Participants may choose to hand stitch the square or use the sewing machine—or a staff member/volunteer can be the designated machine stitcher.

7. Turn the square right-side out, and iron in a 1/4" crease. Then hand- stitch or machine-stitch the final side (a staff member/volunteer can be the designated ironer as deemed necessary).

8. At 1/2" from each corner on one side of the square, cut a small hole in both pieces of fabric one half inch from the top. Put the grommet in place and, with the hammer, lightly tap both pieces together.

9. Take 2 1/2 inches of twine, feed it through each grommet, and tie it around the stick so that fabric swatch hangs from the stick.

10. Continue tying on squares in this fashion until there is at least 2–3 inches of bare stick left on either side.

11. Finally, cut a length of string double the length of the stick (if you have a 6-inch stick with one square on it, use 12 inches of string). Tie each end of the string around the ends of the stick, forming a hanger.

Modifications

Physical
Visual Impairment, Parkinson's, Stroke, MS CP: Visually describe the project and the materials. Have these participants select the fabric through touch and their available vision, if any. For participants with neurological symptoms (tremors, aphasia) have a staff member/volunteer do the actual cutting and use hand signals to indicate choices and desires.

Cognitive
Dementia: The cutting part of this program works very well with dementia—they will cut squares all after noon! Use the rest of the program as a follow-up. Stitch the squares and grommet them yourself (or better yet, recruit a volunteer), then take the squares back to complete the hangers with the dementia group.

Safety Issues

Hot Iron
It is strongly recommended that a staff member/ volunteer be assigned to do any ironing.

Pin Pokes

Be very careful if any participant is Hepatitis-C positive! Rubber fingers may alleviate some accidental pricks and pokes.

Tips and Tricks

- Ask for fabric donations—there is always some discouraged or tired sewer out there who is willing to drop off bundles of pieces. You can use any size of fabric. The suggested size is just that—suggested. This is a good place to start, then use your imagination!

- If making larger squares, consider using pre-made appliqués to stitch or iron onto the squares. Use the iron and heat-bonding hem tape—it is a great timesaver with appliqués!

- Use anything to hang the squares on: old wooden rulers (use alphabet appliqués for a school house theme), a fishing pole (make fish shapes instead of squares), a golf club—the possibilities are endless.

SECTION 5

CREATIVE ARTS

Whether it is through formal poetry, freestyle poetry, descriptive writing, or using pure imagination, these programs foster creativity and self-expression. The setting is almost always intimate. It is an opportunity to connect on a deeper, emotional level with your participants. Hands-on sensory stimulation to self-exploratory writing—each of these programs foster emotional health, safety, and trust-building. The experience can be exhilarating or it can be humbling. Either way, it is a privilege to enter into such personal moments with your participants, so enjoy every moment.

SENSORY THERAPY KIT

Objective

To use interactive therapy to stimulate the senses

Targeted Domains and Benefits

Physical	decreased muscle contracture, decreased muscle tension
Cognitive	promoting relaxation, stimulating long-term memory
Emotional	intrinsic response to familiar smells, textures, and objects, decreasing anxiety

Preparation and Materials

- a small container with dry mixture of 4 cups rice, 4 cups macaroni
- a rain stick (check with a music store, or one can be crafted)
- 6 packages of incense—each scent marked on the package
- 3 small containers of bath salts
- 7 scented hand creams
- 2 small squish balls (stress balls)
- a large multi-colored squish ball
- a feather duster
- a container of scented bubble bath
- a small jar of coffee grounds
- a spiny ball
- a wrist-band with bells
- a set of fabric swatches
- 2 vials of different scented body oils
- a package cotton balls
- a glass jar of eucalyptus leaves

Procedure During Session

1. Sensory stimulation utilizes all, or as many of the five senses as possible. This particular kit concentrates on touch, hearing, sight,

and smell. Program implementation and risk factors are given for each element in the kit.

2. When using this kit with late stage Alzheimer's participants, it is best to facilitate the program on either a 1:1 basis, or in a small group setting with a maximum of three participants. The group could be expanded to four participants with a staff member/ volunteer assisting. Please read the procedure and the risk factors associated with each item.

3. When using the kit with mild to medium impairments, include conversational methods in a reminiscing style to facilitate greater cognitive conditioning.

Procedure

1. In instances in which participant movement (e.g., grasping) is required and the participant is unable to independently participate, the facilitator should place his or her own hands over top of the participant's to assist in producing the required action.

2. Ensure that the participants' hands are washed prior to and after the program.

3. Between individual activities, have participants inhale the scent of the coffee grounds to clear the olfactory senses and prevent a previous scent from influencing a new scent.

Macaroni/Rice Mixture

Have participants place their hands into the small container, ensuring that as much of the hand (up to the wrist) is immersed as possible. If participants require assistance, place their hands in the kit for them and, keeping your hands over top of theirs, initiate the following movements: scoop the material into the hands, then lift the hands and let the material slide through their fingers. Repeat this process at least five times. As the material falls through the fingers back into the container, it creates a gentle, soothing sound similar to rain.

Rain Stick (large, brightly colored cylinder)

Have participants grasp the rain-stick in the middle with both hands and use a twisting wrist motion to turn it from top to bottom, as you would an hourglass timer. The plastic beads mimic the sound of rain and the colors will attract the participants' eyes. The actual manipulation of the stick itself aids participants in improving manual dexterity (grasping) and with ROM in the wrists.

Incense Packages

Each package should have a different scent with their names marked on the outside. I suggest vanilla, cinnamon, sandalwood, lemon, rose, and orange. The scent is often strong enough that the package itself can be left closed and smelled through the plastic.

Bath Salts

Use bath salts with the ingredients listed on the label. Unscrew the cap and, placing the opening slightly below the participants' noses, encourage inhalation.

Scented Hand Cream

Collect a variety of creams, each with a different scent. This portion of the materials should be used primarily in a 1:1 situation. Take off each cap, place the opened cream close to participant's nose, and encourage inhalation. Give a relaxing hand massage with a specific scent, if the participant is able to identify their favorite. If participants are unable to identify their favorite scent, choose which scent will be used. The hand cream should be applied directly to participants' hands and gently massaged into them over a five to ten minute period by the facilitator. The massage can include the forearm (up to elbow) as well, if desired.

Small Squish Balls

Each ball should have a slightly different texture. Ensure that the size of the ball allows for easy grasping and that the firmness increases the amount of pressure required to squeeze it. If the participant cannot grasp or squeeze the ball, the facilitator should place his or her hand over top of the participant's hand and manipulate the hand movement to assist the participant in feeling the texture and, if applicable, aiding in the squeezing motion.

Large Squish Ball

This should be a large, brightly colored ball. Place it in front of participant on a table, or on the lap. Encourage participant to pick up the ball on his or her own. If the participant cannot self-direct, the facilitator can place the ball directly into the participant's hand and encourage further exploration through texture and squeezing. If participants are unable to initiate these movements on their own, the facilitator can assist in manipulating the ball by using the method described for the smaller squish balls.

Feather Duster

Take the feather duster and place the feathered ends into the participant's palm. Encourage a stroking motion in order to feel the texture and smoothness of the feathers. Alternatively, the facilitator can take the duster and lightly "dust" the participant's hands (palm and backs), their face, their arms, and so on.

Scented Bubble Bath

Use an empty plastic ice cream pail or some sort of plastic container with a flat bottom. Fill the container with hot water and add enough bath foam to produce foamy bubbles (approximately three capfuls). Ensure that the scent is strong enough to smell and place the bucket on the table. This will produce a soothing, subtle background scent while working with the tactile elements in the kit. Another option is to use the water to do a hand-soak and massage. Encourage the participant to splash the water with fingertips—this creates a sounds similar to a creek.

Small Jar of Coffee Grounds

Use this item in between each "smelling" element in order to clear the olfactory senses. This clearing allows each new scent to be smelled in a pure form, without any interference from previous smells. The coffee grounds are also a good smell on their own, as the smell of coffee is a familiar one.

Koosh Ball

Turn the participant's hand so that the palm is facing up. Grasp the plastic handle on the ball and gently bounce the ball up and down, touching the palm with each bounce. This procedure can be repeated for the backs of the hands, the face, the arms, the neck, and so on. Place the ball in the participant's palm and encourage manipulation. If the participant is unable to initiate independent actions, the facilitator can cover the participant's hand with his or her own and initiate manipulation in that way. One benefit of facilitator-enhanced manipulation is that of personal touch between the facilitator and the participant. This is an added bonus to the other sensations created by the ball.

Wrist Band With Bells

Place the wristband on the participant's strongest and most mobile side. Each individual movement the participant enacts will produce a soft, tinkling bell sound. The wristband can be used independently of the other elements, or in conjunction with them. Alternatively, the band can be placed around a participant's ankle, or around the toes/ball of the foot if the participant is wearing shoes and if the lower extremities move more easily than the upper extremities.

Fabric Swatch Set

Create a variety of fabrics to be stored in a large Ziploc bag. Have participants select individual swatches to be placed either in front of them or into their palms. Encourage stroking motions both with and against the grain.

This allows exposure to the textures of the fabrics and can produce a strong tactile impression. If the participant is unable to manipulate movements in this way, the facilitator can take the individual swatch and move it across the participant's hands, face, arms, and so on in order to produce the tactile stimulation.

Vials of Scented Oil and Cotton Balls

Each vial of oil should have a definite scent. If the vials do not have labels, identify them by using a sticker. Lightly soak a cotton ball in each of the scents and place them individually under the participant's nose to smell. In addition to smelling, the oil on the cotton ball can be spread onto the hands of the participant and gently massaged in. This will produce a subtle aroma as well as the benefit from touch interaction between the participant and the facilitator. Dispose of all cotton balls after each session.

Glass Jar of Eucalyptus Leaves

Open the jar and wave it just under the participant's nose. If the scent is not strong enough, simply reach into the jar and crush one or two leaves. This will produce a strong, pungent smell that is more easily detected.

Modifications

Physical
For any physical condition: The facilitator will have to assist in manipulation, or create the stimulation through their own movements.

Cognitive
Dementia: This program works exceptionally well with late stage Alzheimer's participants. I have seen participants with a strong contracture sufficiently relaxed enough through this program that the contractured limb stayed in a relaxed condition for a significant amount of time postprogram.

Safety Issues

- Be aware of any allergies—this is very important!
- There is a potential risk of overstimulation if using all the elements in the kit. Knowledge of participant tolerance is important. If participants are not able to verbalize any discomfort, the facilitator must watch for physical signs of discomfort.
- Always wash your own hands and those of the participants before and after each session.
- When using incense sticks, have participants smell them through the plastic package. Actual contact between the incense stick and

the skin will cause a burning sensation. In the event of contact, wipe the area immediately with a mild soap and wet cloth.

- When using bath salts or coffee grounds, ensure that none of the material is inhaled. In the event the material spills onto the participant, dust if off immediately and wash down with a damp cloth. To avoid spillage, cover the mouth of the jar with cheesecloth and secure with a rubber band.

- Ensure that the koosh ball and squishy balls are never placed in participant's mouth.

- Always cap the vials of oil immediately after soaking the cotton ball and dispose of the cotton ball after each individual use.

- Always cap the hand cream immediately after use to prevent spillage and/or ingestion by the participant. In the event of spillage, wipe up the excess with a dry cloth. In the event of ingestion, make nursing staff aware of the occurrence and encourage participants to drink water.

- When using the rain stick, watch for potentially violent expression. Ensure there is no striking of other participants, or of themselves, while using the stick.

- Ensure that the bell wristband securely attached. If attached to the wrist, make sure the bells do not enter the mouth.

- Be aware that fabric swatches may remind some participants of handkerchiefs

Tips and Tricks

- Leave the store hanger tag on the koosh ball to allow it bounce in your hand.

- Use donated baby-food jars to use for the glass jars. The lids are very tight!

- Use donated fabric to make the swatches—and you thought you would never find a use for bright green and pink flowered fabric!

- Ask family/staff members to purchase some of these items for you—most are not very expensive, and if you receive doubles you then have backup for when kit materials need to be replaced.

- This is one of my favorite programs to use with my end-stage Alzheimer's residents. Based on the measurable observation of contracture release, I would work this program in conjunction with physical therapy.

Poetry (Haiku)

Objective

To provide an opportunity for personal expression through the creation of personal poetry

Targeted Domains and Benefits

Physical	fine motor skills, manual dexterity
Cognitive	fostering imagination, following directions/ guidelines
Emotional	emotional outlet to express intrinsic feelings

Preparation and Materials

- a pen or pencil per person
- lined writing paper
- an eraser
- photocopied directions

Procedure

1. Seat the participants around a small table.
2. Read the guidelines for writing Haiku. Facilitators should read aloud a sample they have created themselves and then have the group break down the sample, following the steps in the directions. This will help the group to better understand the concept of Haiku.
3. Work through the directions one line at a time.
4. After the first exercise, have the group write a second poem and try to keep the prompting/cueing by the staff members/volunteers to a minimum. Allow at least fifteen minutes for the group to complete their second poem.
5. When the poems are finished, ask if each participant would like to share their poem and then have a five minute discussion about each participant's poem.

Modifications

Physical
Inability to write (whether due to physical condition or illiteracy): Assign

a staff member/volunteer to scribe for that participant. It is important that the person assisting does not do the thinking for the participant, but merely provides suggestion and encouragement.

Cognitive
This program is best used with a mid to high-functioning group. A mid-range functioning group will require more prompting and cueing.

Safety Issues

Know Your Participants
If one or more of your participants is illiterate, plan for this ahead of time by assigning an assistant who can help those participants work through the exercise with success.

Tips and Tricks

- This is a great exercise to combine with an art group. Have participants create a painting or other piece of artwork and then write Haiku about their artwork. You can display both the artwork and the poetry together in a "gallery showcase."
- Use duotangs filled with lined paper to make inexpensive journals, and each participant uses their own book week after week.
- The ideal group size is four to six participants—this allows for increased intimacy in the group. It also allows staff members/volunteers to provide greater 1:1 interaction within the group.
- Remember to refresh the group's memory about syllables prior to beginning your first group. Use a few general words and have each participant break the words down into syllables as practice.

Haiku Directions

Haiku poems consist of three written lines. The first line contains five syllables, the second line contains seven syllables, and the third line contains five syllables.

Haiku is meant to contain seasonal representation (e.g., use the word "snow" to indicate winter). As the group becomes more experienced in writing Haiku, this particularity can be put into practice.

Example 1
Snow crunches loudly
Bundled up but still so cold
Light in window, home.

Example 2
Canopy of trees
Raindrops sneaking through the leaves
My own secret place

ROLE-REVERSAL FAIRY TALES

Objective

To stimulate imagination while using short-term and long-term memory

Targeted Domains and Benefits

Physical	fine motor skills, manual dexterity
Cognitive	fostering imagination, writing a story in a logical progression

Preparation and Materials

- a pen or pencil with eraser per person
- lined writing paper
- fairy tale books

Procedure

1. Seat participants around a table, ensuring that all participants can hear the facilitator clearly.
2. Have participants make a selection from the fairy tale books the facilitator has brought to the program.
3. Read through the original story and then discuss how that story would change if the bad guy was actually a hero given a bad rap (I usually use the three little pigs for this example). Really work on the cueing and prompting when discussing how the story would change, as this can alleviate groups from stalling when they are trying to write their own versions.
4. Either as a large group, or by splitting the group into pairs, have each group pick a story to read and then reverse. Cue and prompt group(s) as necessary.
5. Allow group(s) maximum time to do their writing—they can use the book as a guide to writing their story, but encourage group(s) to change as much of the story outlook as possible. It is best if the group(s) can finish their story in one program while the creative juices are still flowing. If need be, the program can be carried over to the following week, with enough time allowed at the beginning to refresh the procedure in everyone's mind and re-read what was written to date.

Modifications

Physical
Inability to write (whether due to physical condition or illiteracy): Assign a staff member/volunteer to scribe for that participant. It is important that the person assisting does not do the thinking for the participant, but merely provides suggestion and encouragement.

Cognitive
This program is best used with a high functioning group. A mid-range functioning group will require more prompting and cueing, but the program can still work well with concentrated efforts by the facilitator.

Safety Issues

Know Your Participants
If one or more participants are illiterate, plan for this ahead of time by assigning an assistant who can help those participants work through the exercise with success.

Tips and Tricks

- This is a great exercise to use in an intergenerational program. Pair up children with your participants—they can create their own reverse-tales picture book using blank paper instead of lined and staple it together!

Story Starters

Sleeping Beauty
- What if sleeping beauty was ugly?
- What if she was not sleeping, but at a plastic surgery and spa place getting treatment from the "witch" (who is really a doctor), and the bumbling prince wrecks her spa treatment?

Little Red Riding Hood
- What if Little Red Riding Hood's father was a big-game hunter and she was a scout?
- What if the wolf was a starving immigrant from a neighboring forest?

Three Billy Goats Gruff
- What if the troll were allergic to sunlight?
- What if the goats didn't even need to use the bridge, but were just being difficult?

Goldilocks
- What if Goldilocks was a spoiled brat?

Rumpelstiltskin
- What if Rumpelstiltskin was really a misunderstood chemist?

Cinderella
- What if Cinderella was ugly and her sisters were beautiful?
- What if the stepmother was trying her best, but Cindy was angry over her parents' divorce?

ALL ABOUT ME

Objective

To stimulate self-reflection using abstract descriptions

Targeted Domains and Benefits

Physical	fine motor skills, manual dexterity
Cognitive	fostering imagination, abstract thought
Emotional	emotional exploration/expression
Spiritual	spiritual essence/beliefs explored and identified

Preparation and Materials

- a pen or pencil with eraser per person
- lined writing paper

Procedure

1. Seat participants around a small table. Ensure that all participants can hear the facilitator clearly.
2. Participants should have enough writing space to keep their work private.
3. Explain the procedure and read aloud a sample poem so that participants understand the goal.
4. Using the supplied outline, work through the steps, as indicated, with the participants.
5. Once the poem is completed, ask the participants to share their poems and have a five-minute discussion about each poem read aloud.

Modifications

Physical
Inability to write (whether due to physical condition or illiteracy): Assign a staff member/volunteer to scribe for that participant. It is important that the person assisting does not do the thinking for the participant, but merely provides suggestion and encouragement.

Cognitive
This program is best used with a high functioning group.

Emotional/Spiritual
Be prepared for latent, negative emotions to arise. Many participants have a hard time focusing on positive analogies versus negative ones during this activity.

Safety Issues

Emotional Health
Negative emotional and spiritual expression may arise during the exercise. Allow participants to write what they feel, as it can be a cathartic experience to release negative views of one's self. If this occurs, discuss the "why" during the discussion period and encourage participants to rewrite numerous poems, each with a progressively more positive aspect.

Tips and Tricks

- Multiple copies of a thesaurus come in handy.
- This is a great exercise to begin a scrapbooking/journaling life history book. Have one of these poems on the front page and after more writings and self-reflection, have participants finish off the last page of their life story with another poem. See how and if anything has changed during the creation of the book. Family members love reading these!

Who Am I?

Line 1: First name/nickname of the person
Line 2: Who is: (three adjectives that describe you)
Line 3: Who enjoys: (list three things you enjoy)
Line 4: Who desires: (list three things you want)
Line 5: (two most important relationships)*
Line 6: Who sees life as: (three words to describe life)
Line 7: Whose dreams are: (list three dreams/goals)**
Line 8: Who's traveled: (three places you have been)**
Line 9: Last name of the person in the poem

* to fill in the relationship line, use the x of y formula, where x is the relationship (e.g., mother of) and y is other party in the relationship.
**You can also substitute "Who's afraid of" for line 7 or 8.

Sample Poem

Jane
Beautiful, patient, silly
Who enjoys hockey, family, friends
Who desires peace, love, and children
Daughter of Penny, aunt of Emma
Who sees life as temporary, meaningful, fleeting
Whose dreams are good health, a happy family, wealth
Who's traveled to Texas, New York, and Ottawa
Smith

CIRCLE WRITING

Objective

To stimulate creativity within a group environment

Targeted Domains and Benefits

Physical	fine motor skills, manual dexterity
Cognitive	fostering imagination, stimulating long/short-term memory
Emotional	emotional exploration/expression, creating emotion within a story context

Preparation and Materials

- a pen or pencil with eraser per person
- lined writing paper

Procedure

1. Seat participants around a small table. Ensure that all participants can hear the facilitator clearly.
2. Have each participant keep track of the supplied words/phrases on their own paper (for easy reference later) or assign a scribe to write them down on a single piece of paper.
3. Starting on the facilitator's left, go around the table and ask each participant for any word or phrase that comes to mind. Allow a fifteen to thirty second response time, then cue the participant as necessary.
4. Work around the table at least twice (when working with a group of four) then stop and try to create the first story. Filler/joiner words and phrases can be added to make the story coherent (but not necessarily sensible!).
5. Try at least two shorter stories (two words/phrases per person) so that participants begin to understand how to link the words/phrases into stories.
6. Once the concept is clearly understood, try a longer story and attempt to make it as logical as possible.

Modifications

Physical
Inability to write (whether due to physical condition or illiteracy): Assign a staff member/volunteer to scribe for that participant. It is important that the person assisting does not do the thinking for the participant, but merely provides suggestion and encouragement.

Cognitive
This program can be used with mid-high range functioning participants.

Emotional
Be prepared for anything from sexually inappropriate comments to harsh negativity. Redirect these participants to a more appropriate word/phrase, or use group consensus to determine whether or not that offering will be accepted by the rest of the group.

Safety Issues

Inappropriate Comments
Outline rules for the words/phrases prior to beginning so that inappropriate comments are less likely to arise.

Tips and Tricks

- Bring a thesaurus and a dictionary!
- I usually scribe the first few efforts and create the filler/joiner words so the participants can follow along with the provided words and see how imagination adds the rest.

Sample Story

Words provided by group: dragon, blue water, fan, chicken, flying, eyes, dolphin, food. Use words in order they were provided.

> The *dragon* lived far beyond the *blue water*. Because the dragon's house was so hot the *fan* was always on, especially when the *chicken* came to visit. You could see the chicken *flying* over once a month on a medical visit to check the dragon's *eyes*. The chicken would even check the health of the pet *dolphin* that lived there with the dragon, and make sure it had enough *food* to eat.

The facilitator can add the filler/joiner words for the first few stories until the participants understand the process—then have the group do a story from start to finish.

COLLAGE IMAGERY

Objective

To stimulate creativity using pictorial materials

Targeted Domains and Benefits

Physical	fine motor skills, manual dexterity
Cognitive	fostering imagination, stimulating long/short-term memory, object selection
Emotional	emotional exploration/expression, creating emotion within a story context

Preparation and Materials

- scissors
- old magazines, calendars, newspapers
- 11 x 17 sheets of paper (one per person)
- glue sticks

Procedure

1. Seat participants in a working area that allows for plenty of elbow room.
2. Outline the program objective to participants: to create a visual representation of themselves using pictures/words/letters found in the provided supplies.
3. Distribute a number of newspapers, magazines, and calendars to the center of each work table. Provide magazines covering a wide variety of topics and interest.
4. Hand out to each participant: one 11 x 17 sheet of blank paper, glue stick, and scissors.
5. Give participants a time frame in which this needs to be completed. Give them a verbal warning when twenty minutes remain. In the last ten minutes, use five minutes to discuss some of the finished pieces, and five minutes for clean up.

Modifications

Physical
Stroke, Parkinson's, Visual Impairment: For visual impairment, assign a staff member/volunteer to visually describe what pictures are available and what type of text participants may want to use to express themselves. If a participant is unable to physically cut or glue independently, assist that participant but ensure that participants make all choices as to what is selected.

Cognitive
Dementia: This program may not meet the exact objective of self-description, but it will reflect these participants' personal interests and usually provides an opportunity to reminisce as well.

Safety Issues

Emotional Outbursts
Be prepared for strong emotional output into this exercise. I have seen great anger and fear expressed using this method, but it can also be very cathartic for the participant. If such as situation arises, professionally assess it and contact members of the interdisciplinary team as deemed appropriate (e.g., social worker, pastoral care).

Tips and Tricks

- Use as wide a variety of printed materials as possible—participants can become a bit testy if someone else uses a picture/letter they wanted to use.
- Check with your local library—they usually cull their collections yearly.
- Put magazines, papers, and calendars on your wish list. You will soon have a larger collection than you have room to store!

Paint Blot

Objective

To stimulate creativity using pictorial materials

Targeted Domains and Benefits

Physical	fine motor skills, manual dexterity
Cognitive	fostering imagination, stimulating long/short-term memory
Emotional	emotional exploration/expression, creating emotion based on art
Spiritual	opportunity to explore personal spirituality through descriptive writing

Preparation and Materials

- a pen or pencil with eraser per person
- lined writing paper
- a paintbrush per person
- paint
- plain paper

Procedure

1. Seat participants in a working area that allows for plenty of elbow room.
2. Distribute a blank sheet of paper and a large paintbrush to each participant.
3. Fold the plain paper in half, then unfold it to be flat once again.
4. Have each participant blob paint onto one half of the paper, using the paint color of their choice
5. With paint on one half of paper, fold the paper again so that the paint is squashed in between the paper and press lightly.
6. Unfold and view the paint blot. This is the artwork that the participant will use to write about.

7. Have each participant study their paint-blot quickly. Using their imagination, they will write about what the object is, what its purpose is, where it came from, and its personality traits.

8. Have the participants repeat steps 3–7, only this time have them pass their artwork to the person on the left and then write about the piece of art they have just received.

Modifications

Physical

This program is not suitable for severe visual impairment. It can be used with glaucoma, early macular degeneration, and cataracts with some verbal descriptions provided for these participants. For neurological or CNS conditions, a scribe may have to be assigned to assist that participant with the writing portion of the program.

Cognitive

Dementia: Writing descriptions about the artwork may be changed to a verbal discussion about each participant's creation—in other words, do the writing verbally. The creation process may be repeated a number of times during the program.

Safety Issues

Negative Emotions

Anger, violence, etc., may be written out when describing artwork. If the writings are perceived to be exceptionally violent or lean toward issues of self-harm, advise other members of the interdisciplinary team immediately to arrange intervention.

Tips and Tricks

- Do not use copious amounts of paint—it takes longer to dry and tends to run out the sides of the folded paper.
- You can frame the artwork along with the written description and then showcase the collection at a "gallery" evening.

10-WORD FRENZY

Objective

To stimulate creativity by using a varied list of words

Targeted Domains and Benefits

Physical	fine motor skills, manual dexterity
Cognitive	positive learning environment, enhancing memory/ understanding
Emotional	emotional exploration/expression through writing
Spiritual	opportunity to explore personal spirituality through descriptive writing

Preparation and Materials

- a pen or pencil with eraser per person
- lined writing paper
- word list

Procedure

1. Seat participants in a working area that allows for plenty of elbow room.
2. Distribute lined paper, pens/pencils, and a word list (of ten words) to each participant.
3. Use a sample list and complete the list as a group so that participants have a clear understanding of the process.
4. Using each word in the list, create a sentence or phrase that includes the word in a contextually correct form.
5. The first sentence will usually determine the direction of the short story.
6. Use the remainder of words on the list, employing the same technique—allow participants the time to think the sentence/phrase through so that each sentence builds on the other to make a coherent story.

7. After the sample exercise is completed, participants will then use the above method and words from their own list to create their short story.

Modifications

Physical
For visual impairment, assign a staff/volunteer to scribe and read words from list. The participants will form their own sentences based on this information. For neurological or CNS conditions, a scribe may have to be assigned to assist that participant with the writing portion of the program.

Cognitive
The program is best suited for high-functioning participants, as the group will need to understand grammar, context, and sequencing.

Safety Issues

Embarrassment
Some participants may be embarrassed or defensive if they do not know or understand the word. Use the word in a sentence to assist them in understanding context and consistently promote the value of learning something new every day.

Tips and Tricks

- If using a sentence to show context, try not to use one that would fit into a participant's story—they will want to use yours instead of creating their own.
- Having a dictionary on hand is vital—my residents ask great questions that I usually have to reference the dictionary to answer!
- Use the dictionary to create a number of word lists—just open the dictionary at random, point a finger and use that word. When creating word lists, number them so that participants do not get the same word list over and over. You can also use these word lists for spelling bees.
- This is a great project for use with a volunteer. Have them create multiple lists that you can simply photocopy as needed, or use words from spelling-bee lists.

Sample Word Lists

List #1

discomfort, malign, porch, signal, talisman, apple, wield, linger, lopsided, idol

List #2

magnanimous, lurch, incentive, gaudy, frigate, dumbfounded, critical, camel, ballast, adhesive

List #3

ailment, dulcet, eminent, congenial, seize, thimble, carve, prehistoric, jumble, kindling

List #4

judicious, knickers, puritan, bourgeoisie, asparagus, wraith, unkempt, vendetta, primal, oak

List #5

scorpion, ratio, larder, patina, glum, oxygen, caffeine, artichoke, spout, terrain

List #6

adhesive, collar, pensive, eggplant, frail, tepid, enchant, islet, drench, complete

List #7

irrational, extraordinary, humble, pleasant, wrath, yodel, anguish, hope, intrinsic, limited

ALL SHAPES AND SIZES

Objective

To stimulate personal exploration by using words and shapes

Targeted Domains and Benefits

Physical	fine motor skills, manual dexterity
Cognitive	learning new vocabulary, stimulating long/short-term memory
Emotional	emotional exploration/expression of self through writing
Spiritual	opportunity to explore personal spirituality through descriptive writing

Preparation and Materials

- a pen or pencil with eraser per person
- lined writing paper
- word list
- a dictionary
- a thesaurus
- sample shapes

Procedure

1. Seat participants in a working area that allows for plenty of elbow room.
2. Distribute pens/pencils to each participant.
3. Review a prepared sample with participants. This will make the process more clearly understood.
4. Explain the procedure to the group. Participants may choose an available sample shape (previously created by the facilitator) or create their own. Using a variety of words (stick to using a maximum of two words instead of whole phrases, and link the words—i.e., life, death, holding hands, etc.), follow the line of the shape until the outline is completely covered. The object is to use words that reflect all parts of the participant.

5. If the group completes the exercise quickly, have each participant complete a second figure.

Modifications

Physical
Visual Impairment, MS, Parkinson's, CP, Brain Injury: In these situations, assign a staff member/volunteer to work with this participant to assist in choosing/drawing a shape and to write the words that participant selects onto their object.

Cognitive
This program is best suited for high-functioning participants, as the group will need to understand grammar, context, and sequencing.

Safety Issues

Embarrassment
Some participants may experience difficulty in finding words that they feel describe themselves, or they may be unable to draw their own shape. Use a word list and have a variety of prepared shapes for such participants.

Tips and Tricks

- It is ideal to have at least one dictionary and thesaurus available for every two participants to share. I use the condensed student version (3-hole punched)—they are less expensive and much easier to cart around than the 20 pound versions!
- Have a staff member/volunteer create multiple word lists of nouns, verbs, and adjectives. The lists do not have to be extensive—ten words is usually enough to generate further thought.
- Use your computer to create generic shapes. You can also photocopy objects, overlay them with a plain piece of paper, and then outline the shapes with a marker. I've traced bunny rabbits, flowers, cars, horses, trees, fruit and more.

Completed Outline Sample (see page 172)

THE 5 W's

Objective

To use inanimate objects to stimulate imagination

Targeted Domains and Benefits

Physical	fine motor skills, manual dexterity
Cognitive	learn new vocabulary, stimulate long-term/short-term memory
Emotional	emotional exploration/expression of self through writing
Spiritual	opportunity to explore personal spirituality through descriptive writing

Preparation and Materials

- a pen or pencil with eraser per person
- lined writing paper
- word list
- a dictionary
- a thesaurus
- an inanimate object/picture

Procedure

1. Seat participants in a working area that allows for plenty of elbow room.
2. Distribute pens/pencils and lined paper to each participant.
3. Take a number of samples from magazines/calendars/newspapers (pictures) or general items (toaster, flowerpot, book) for the group to select from.
4. Use a sample object in a group exercise to assist participants in understanding the concept clearly.
5. Each participant will select a picture or object.
6. Have the five W's written out for participants to follow: Who, What, Where, When, Why, and add How as an added measure. Using

these prompts, have participants create imaginary information about their object/picture.

7. Once the basic questions are filled in, work through the six headings and add more details (point form works well).

8. After adding more details, each participant will use their details in order to create short story about their object/picture.

Modifications

Physical

Visual Impairment, MS, Parkinson's, CP, Brain Injury: In these situations, assign a staff member/volunteer to work with these participants to scribe for them. The participants will provide the details while the staff member/volunteer cues/prompts only as necessary.

Cognitive

This program is best suited for high-functioning participants, as the group will need to understand grammar, context, and sequencing. If using with dementia participants, substitute the writing for oral ideas. The facilitator can make point form notes and then "spin" the story back to the participants.

Safety Issues

Self-Doubt

This may be a strange exercise for participants not used to writing and using imagination. Use one or more samples to involve the group creatively and to stimulate imagination. Be verbally supportive and creatively helpful in order to facilitate success.

Tips and Tricks

- Physical items for "animation" work best if familiar: toaster, car, animals, people (the pictures can provide immediate interpretations in body language), and trees.

- If participants are having difficulty, draw an analogy to fairy tales where animals, etc. have been given personalities.

- A great program to use in an intergenerational setting. Create teams—the kids provide much of the creativity, the participants follow their lead, and much hilarity ensues!

Appendix

FUNNY MONEY

$5000 funny money
insert picture of choice here

$10,000 funny money
insert picture of choice here

$25,000 funny money
insert picture of choice here

$50,000 funny money
insert picture of choice here

$50 funny money
insert picture of choice here

$100 funny money
insert picture of choice here

$500 funny money
insert picture of choice here

$1000 funny money
insert picture of choice here

BLANK CHECKS

Your Facility Here   Date_____ 20_____

Pay to the order of _____ $ _____

_____ /00 Dollars

Bank of Brilliance
5555 IQ Avenue
Anywhere, WorldWide   _____

Your Facility Here   Date_____ 20_____

Pay to the order of _____ $ _____

_____ /00 Dollars

Bank of Brilliance
5555 IQ Avenue
Anywhere, WorldWide   _____

Your Facility Here   Date_____ 20_____

Pay to the order of _____ $ _____

_____ /00 Dollars

Bank of Brilliance
5555 IQ Avenue
Anywhere, WorldWide   _____

Your Facility Here   Date_____ 20_____

Pay to the order of _____ $ _____

_____ /00 Dollars

Bank of Brilliance
5555 IQ Avenue
Anywhere, WorldWide   _____

Game 1: Canada

In each column, question numbers are followed by the jelly bean reward amount in parentheses.

Geography		Provincial/Territorial Capitals	Famous Canadians	Famous Canadian Events
1. (2)		1. (2)	1. (2)	1. (2)
2. (4)	Team One	2. (4)	2. (4)	2. (4)
3. (5)		3. (5)	3. (5)	3. (5)
4. (6)	Team One	4. (6)	4. (6)	4. (6)
5. (7)	Team One	5. (7)	5. (7)	5. (7)
6. (8)		6. (8)	6. (8)	6. (8)
7. (10)	Team Two	7. (10)	7. (10)	7. (10)
8. (12)		8. (12)	8. (12)	8. (12)
9. (14)	Team Two	9. (14)	9. (14)	9. (14)
10. (15)		10. (15)	10. (15)	10. (15)

Example of whiteboard with game in progress (five questions have been answered under the first category), with Team winners listed and current jellybean count: Team One (17 jellybeans), Team Two (24 jellybeans).

Elf Blocks Pattern Cutouts

ARMS

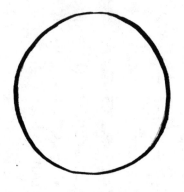

COLLAR

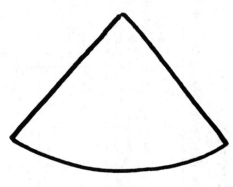

HAT

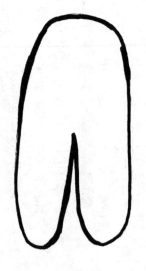

PANTS

PROGRESSION OF LAYERS

TIN LID HOLE PUNCHING LAYOUTS

How To Use Statistics Sheet for Ongoing Evaluation

Key Points

- Create this form in Microsoft Word—it will need to be updated monthly.

- In order not to waste paper or accidentally "lose" stat sheets, print off new sheets only at the end of every month. In the event that a person arrives at/leaves the facility, write their name in pencil (on the same line as the first person) under the date they arrived/left. In the event of a death discharge, color in a rectangle (on that person's line), crossing the vertical line after their last participation date (see sample).

- Use a maximum of two units per sheet—it's faster to tally the month's end that way.

- View the sample sheet. If you consistently and accurately fill out these statistic sheets every day, the sheet can be read at any given moment, which allows you to:
    - Check indicators on decreasing/increasing participation levels for each person, each program, and each unit.
    - Assess if a new/old program is indicated as a success or a less-of-a-success.
    - Have an accurate representation of each participant's diet at your fingertips.
    - Assess the success of a single program, as it is run in different time blocks (comparative).
    - Determine if an existing participant is exhibiting indicators that call for a reassessment or discharge from the program (decreasing participation, behaviors, change in physical condition).

Option: Daily outside temperatures can be added as side notes, to help track how weather affects attendance, participation levels, and behaviors.

How to Read the Sample Statistics Sheet

Assume the numbers for these programs (same time, same day, same unit) have been indicated, as in the sample sheet, for three concurrent months. You can then determine that:

criteria specific (ladies)

MONTH Jan. '05		7 music	8 crafts	9 nail care	10 pet visits	11 chapel	12 crafts	13 baking	14 music	15 puzzles	16 music	17 movies
Name: Susie Unit: 10-Y												
1. Bob	P/F2	✓	✓		✓							
2. Bill	CU	S			✓							
3. Margaret		S		✓	✓							
4. Sam	P	✓	✓		✓							
5. Tyler	NAS	✓			✓							
6. Linda		O	✓L	S	✓							
7. Sally		I	I	I■ ← indicates death								
8. Grace	M	✓		✓	✓							
9. Mary	P	✓		✓	✓							
10. Joe	P	✓ P			O							
11. Tina	CU	S			✓							
12. Ella	CU	✓			✓							
13. Tom		✓L	✓		✓							
14. Jeff	CU	R	R		S							
15. Agnes		F		✓	✓							
16. Edith		✓		✓	✓							
17. Anne	M	✓		R	R							
18. Shirley	TF	R	R	S	✓							
19. Ted		R			✓							
20. Frank	P/F1	✓X			✓							
21. Dan		✓	✓		✓							
22. Elizabeth		✓		✓	✓							
23. Archie	CU	R			S							
24. Dick	M	✓			✓							
TOTALS		10	4	6	19							

Indicators

Activity Code
A - Active
P - Passive
S - Sleeping
I - Ill
L - Left early
F - Family/visitors
O - Out
R - Refused
X - Agitated

Diets
NAS - No added sugar
M - Minced
CU -cutup
P - Pureed
TF - Tube feed
D - Diabetic
V - Vegetarian
RE - Renal diet, no added salt, low fluids. Check with nsg. re: serving

Fluid Levels
F1 - Level one
F2 - Level two
F3 - Level three

■ - Death

- Your craft program needs to be changed. Try a different time of day, a different day entirely, and reassess what crafts you have been using. (Has cognition changed? Do the craft instructions contain too many steps?), and assess post-changes at a selected time (i.e., four weeks, twelve weeks?).

- Shirley (room 18) has a strong response to pets but displays no interest in large-group programs.

- The pet-visits program appears to be working very well. Perhaps increase the number of times the pets visit in a week?
- Sally (room 7) was seriously ill and then passed away. Write the name of the new participant in the boxes immediately behind the death indicator.
- Frank (room 20) has been consistently agitated in music programs but there are no other program agitations are noted. Reassess as to his suitability of participation and query: Does he need new hearing aids? Does he have "Sundowners"? Will a 1:1 intervention during a music program assist in keeping him in the program longer?
- There are blanks where no indicators are written. Query if the recreation staff is asking/inviting all participants in the unit to the program? (an exception would be a criteria specific program such as nail care/painting). How are they encouraging attendance? (this is a good heads up to troubleshoot potential performance issues within your staff).

These are just a few examples of what these statistical tracking sheets can tell you in a glance, IF they are filled out consistently and accurately.

How to Fill Out the Statistical Tracking Sheet

- Fill in the corresponding month (include the year—it prevents confusion a year or two later!). It is also a good practice to keep each year's statistics (individual units and monthly tabulations) in their own binder.
- Recreation staff members fill in their names on their statistic sheets only.
- Indicate the location from which the statistics have been collected (i.e., if your unit is called A2, then that would be the unit indicator).
- As shown in the sample, write the date and the program in the large boxes (total of 10 across) on the top of the page (use as many of these sheets as required in a month).
- Ensure that the lists are as up-to-date as possible—with correct names and diets/fluids—at the end of each month.
- Using check marks and the supplied indicators (activity, diet, fluids) track each participant's individual progress on a daily basis.
- *All* participant boxes should be checked off. If they are not being checked off and many blanks are being left, check with your staff. This could indicate a need to problem-solve with staff members for ways to increase floor performance.
- Print out as many sheets as you will require for *all* your programs for the month.

This type of statistical tracking is invaluable—not only as an on going process to assist the development and building of your recreation department, but it is also worth its weight in gold when used in care conferences, family meetings, and budget meetings:

Conferences/Family Meetings

- Can provide consistent and ongoing participation levels: degree of involvement, type of involvement (frequency and program type), documentation record supporting adding/decreasing specific programs into a participant's care plan.
- Relieves family concerns regarding quality of life and recreational involvement.
- Can also support a request for additional funds for participants with public guardians (sample query: I would suggest exploring a paid companion, because as you can see here [show collected statistics] Mrs. Z consistently refuses participation in our programs but does well with her volunteer visitor. However, the volunteer visitor can only come once every two weeks).

Budget Meetings

- Creates a benchmark of existing numbers of participants served with current staffing levels.
- Written documentation of increased direct-patient-care time when comparing months (i.e., summer months with a summer student versus regular staffing levels).

The monthly tally sheet allows for all programs to be written out and for specific participation levels (direct-patient-care time) to be indicated as both units and total facility. On the sample sheet, there are unit-specific totals as well as accumulated (whole facility) numbers (using four units as a base). For clarity's sake, I have my assistants break our numbers down further by listing our regular calendar events and then our "special events." It is up to each Recreation department to determine if the "special events" designation applies, but my department classifies "special events" as those events requiring more than any one recreation staff to implement (e.g., large group music programs, summer barbecues, etc., including programs which only require one assistant but also the presence of the recreation therapist). It may sound time-consuming, but if you implement and continue this tracking, it becomes second nature and takes only minutes a day. Remember the golden rule: *If it is not written down, it never happened!*

Other Books by Venture Publishing, Inc.

21st Century Leisure: Current Issues, Second Edition
   by Valeria J. Freysinger and John R. Kelly
The A•B•Cs of Behavior Change: Skills for Working With Behavior Problems in Nursing Homes
   by Margaret D. Cohn, Michael A. Smyer, and Ann L. Horgas
Activity Experiences and Programming within Long-Term Care
   by Ted Tedrick and Elaine R. Green
The Activity Gourmet
   by Peggy Powers
Advanced Concepts for Geriatric Nursing Assistants
   by Carolyn A. McDonald
Adventure Programming
   edited by John C. Miles and Simon Priest
Assessment: The Cornerstone of Activity Programs
   by Ruth Perschbacher
Behavior Modification in Therapeutic Recreation: An Introductory Manual
   by John Datillo and William D. Murphy
Benefits of Leisure
   edited by B. L. Driver, Perry J. Brown, and George L. Peterson
Benefits of Recreation Research Update
   by Judy M. Sefton and W. Kerry Mummery
Beyond Baskets and Beads: Activities for Older Adults With Functional Impairments
   by Mary Hart, Karen Primm, and Kathy Cranisky
Beyond Bingo: Innovative Programs for the New Senior
   by Sal Arrigo, Jr., Ann Lewis, and Hank Mattimore
Beyond Bingo 2: More Innovative Programs for the New Senior
   by Sal Arrigo, Jr.
Both Gains and Gaps: Feminist Perspectives on Women's Leisure
   by Karla Henderson, M. Deborah Bialeschki, Susan M. Shaw, and Valeria J. Freysinger
Boredom Busters: Themed Special Events to Dazzle and Delight Your Group
   by Annette C. Moore
Client Assessment in Therapeutic Recreation Services
   by Norma J. Stumbo
Client Outcomes in Therapeutic Recreation Services
   by Norma J. Stumbo
Conceptual Foundations for Therapeutic Recreation
   edited by David R. Austin, John Datillo, and Bryan P. McCormick
Constraints to Leisure
   edited by Edgar L. Jackson
Dementia Care Programming: An Identity-Focused Approach
   by Rosemary Dunne
Dimensions of Choice: A Qualitative Approach to Recreation, Parks, and Leisure Research
   by Karla A. Henderson
Diversity and the Recreation Profession: Organizational Perspectives
   edited by Maria T. Allison and Ingrid E. Schneider
Effective Management in Therapeutic Recreation Service
   by Gerald S. O'Morrow and Marcia Jean Carter
Evaluating Leisure Services: Making Enlightened Decisions, Second Edition
   by Karla A. Henderson and M. Deborah Bialeschki
Everything From A to Y: The Zest Is up to You! Older Adult Activities for Every Day of the Year
   by Nancy R. Cheshire and Martha L. Kenney
The Evolution of Leisure: Historical and Philosophical Perspectives
   by Thomas Goodale and Geoffrey Godbey
Experience Marketing: Strategies for the New Millennium
   by Ellen L. O'Sullivan and Kathy J. Spangler
Facilitation Techniques in Therapeutic Recreation
   by John Datillo

File o' Fun: A Recreation Planner for Games & Activities, Third Edition
    by Jane Harris Ericson and Diane Ruth Albright
Functional Interdisciplinary-Transdisciplinary Therapy (FITT) Manual
    by Deborah M. Schott, Judy D. Burdett, Beverly J. Cook, Karren S. Ford, and Kathleen M. Orban
The Game and Play Leader's Handbook: Facilitating Fun and Positive Interaction, Revised Edition
    by Bill Michaelis and John M. O'Connell
The Game Finder—A Leader's Guide to Great Activities
    by Annette C. Moore
Getting People Involved in Life and Activities: Effective Motivating Techniques
    by Jeanne Adams
Glossary of Recreation Therapy and Occupational Therapy
    by David R. Austin
Great Special Events and Activities
    by Annie Morton, Angie Prosser, and Sue Spangler
Group Games & Activity Leadership
    by Kenneth J. Bulik
Growing With Care: Using Greenery, Gardens, and Nature With Aging and Special Populations
    by Betsy Kreidler
Hands On! Children's Activities for Fairs, Festivals, and Special Events
    by Karen L. Ramey
In Search of the Starfish: Creating a Caring Environment
    by Mary Hart, Karen Primm, and Kathy Cranisky
Inclusion: Including People With Disabilities in Parks and Recreation Opportunities
    by Lynn Anderson and Carla Brown Kress
Inclusive Leisure Services: Responding to the Rights of People with Disabilities, Second Edition
    by John Dattilo
Innovations: A Recreation Therapy Approach to Restorative Programs
    by Dawn R. De Vries and Julie M. Lake
Internships in Recreation and Leisure Services: A Practical Guide for Students, Third Edition
    by Edward E. Seagle, Jr. and Ralph W. Smith
Interpretation of Cultural and Natural Resources, Second Edition
    by Douglas M. Knudson, Ted T. Cable, and Larry Beck
Intervention Activities for At-Risk Youth
    by Norma J. Stumbo
Introduction to Outdoor Recreation: Providing and Managing Natural Resource Based Opportunities
    by Roger L. Moore and B. L. Driver
Introduction to Recreation and Leisure Services, Eighth Edition
    by Karla A. Henderson, M. Deborah Bialeschki, John L. Hemingway, Jan S. Hodges, Beth D. Kivel, and H. Douglas Sessoms
Introduction to Therapeutic Recreation: U.S. and Canadian Perspectives
    by Kenneth Mobily and Lisa Ostiguy
Introduction to Writing Goals and Objectives: A Manual for Recreation Therapy Students and Entry-Level Professionals
    by Suzanne Melcher
Leadership and Administration of Outdoor Pursuits, Second Edition
    by Phyllis Ford and James Blanchard
Leadership in Leisure Services: Making a Difference, Second Edition
    by Debra J. Jordan
Leisure and Leisure Services in the 21st Century
    by Geoffrey Godbey
The Leisure Diagnostic Battery: Users Manual and Sample Forms
    by Peter A. Witt and Gary Ellis
Leisure Education I: A Manual of Activities and Resources, Second Edition
    by Norma J. Stumbo
Leisure Education II: More Activities and Resources, Second Edition
    by Norma J. Stumbo

Research in Therapeutic Recreation: Concepts and Methods
    edited by Marjorie J. Malkin and Christine Z. Howe
Simple Expressions: Creative and Therapeutic Arts for the Elderly in Long-Term Care Facilities
    by Vicki Parsons
A Social History of Leisure Since 1600
    by Gary Cross
A Social Psychology of Leisure
    by Roger C. Mannell and Douglas A. Kleiber
Special Events and Festivals: How to Organize, Plan, and Implement
    by Angie Prosser and Ashli Rutledge
Stretch Your Mind and Body: Tai Chi as an Adaptive Activity
    by Duane A. Crider and William R. Klinger
Therapeutic Activity Intervention with the Elderly: Foundations and Practices
    by Barbara A. Hawkins, Marti E. May, and Nancy Brattain Rogers
Therapeutic Recreation and the Nature of Disabilities
    by Kenneth E. Mobily and Richard D. MacNeil
Therapeutic Recreation: Cases and Exercises, Second Edition
    by Barbara C. Wilhite and M. Jean Keller
Therapeutic Recreation in Health Promotion and Rehabilitation
    by John Shank and Catherine Coyle
Therapeutic Recreation in the Nursing Home
    by Linda Buettner and Shelley L. Martin
Therapeutic Recreation Programming: Theory and Practice
    by Charles Sylvester, Judith E. Voelkl, and Gary D. Ellis
Therapeutic Recreation Protocol for Treatment of Substance Addictions
    by Rozanne W. Faulkner
The Therapeutic Recreation Stress Management Primer
    by Cynthia Mascott
The Therapeutic Value of Creative Writing
    by Paul M. Spicer
Tourism and Society: A Guide to Problems and Issues
    by Robert W. Wyllie
Traditions: Improving Quality of Life in Caregiving
    by Janelle Sellick

Venture Publishing, Inc.
1999 Cato Avenue
State College, PA 16801
Phone: (814) 234-4561
Fax: (814) 234-1651

Date Due

OCT 11 2011		
NOV 03 2011		
NOV 26 2012		
MAY 17 2013		
MAY 07 2013		